EZRA POUND
Purpose/Form/Meaning

MARIANNE KORN
PhD BA B LITT

MIDDLESEX POLYTECHNIC PRESS
PEMBRIDGE PRESS

8 / / x
C . 2

©Marianne Korn 1983
Published for Middlesex Polytechnic Press by Pembridge Press Ltd, 16 Pembridge
Road, London W11, and printed and bound in the UK by Redwood Burn Ltd,
Trowbridge, Wiltshire.

First published 1983

British Library Cataloguing in Publication Data

Korn, Marianne
    Ezra Pound.
    1. Pound, Ezra—Criticism and interpretation
    I. Title
    811'.52   PS3531.082Z/

    ISBN 0-86206-008-7

Typeset by Allset Composition in 10 on 11 point Press Roman

CONTENTS

ACKNOWLEDGEMENTS

Thanks are due to the British Academy (Small Grants in the Humanities) and to Middlesex Polytechnic for assistance, in the form of money and time, toward the completion of the book; to the librarians at the Beinecke Library (New Haven) especially, for their help and unfailing courtesy; to Donald Gallup and Mary de Rachewiltz for their kindness; and above all to my family and friends, who had to live through it.

Permission to quote from the following works of Ezra Pound has been granted by Faber & Faber Ltd, London, and the New Directions Publishing Corporation, New York: *Collected shorter poems* (*Personae* in the United States) – Copyright 1926 by the Trustees of the Ezra Pound Literary Property Trust. *A lume spento* © 1965 Ezra Pound. *The Cantos of Ezra Pound* © 1975 The Ezra Pound Literary Property Trust. *Selected letters 1907-1941*, edited by D D Paige – Copyright 1950 by the Trustees of the Ezra Pound Literary Property Trust. *Selected prose 1909-1965*, edited by William Cookson – Copyright © 1973 by the Trustees of the Ezra Pound Literary Property Trust. *The literary essays of Ezra Pound* – Copyright 1918, 1930, 1935 by the Trustees of the Ezra Pound Literary Property Trust. *Active anthology*, edited by Ezra Pound – Copyright 1933 by the Trustees of the Ezra Pound Literary Property Trust. *Translations* – Copyright © 1963 by the Trustees of the Ezra Pound Literary Property Trust. *Polite essays* – Copyright 1937 by the Trustees of the Ezra Pound Literary Property Trust. *Gaudier-Brzeska: A memoir* – Copyright © 1970 by the Trustees of the Ezra Pound Literary Property Trust. *ABC of reading* – Copyright 1934 by the Trustees of the Ezra Pound Literary Property Trust. Finally, from various uncollected essays in *TP's weekly, Vortex, Little review, Criterion, Poetry, New English weekly, New age, English journal* and many other short extracts – Copyright © 1983 by the Trustees of the Ezra Pound Literary Property Trust.

Thanks are also due to Peter Owen Ltd for permission to quote from the following: *The spirit of romance* (revised edition), Peter Owen Ltd, London, 1952; *Guide to kulchur*, New Directions, Norfolk, Conn, nd; *Patria mia and The treatise on harmony*, Peter Owen Ltd, London, 1962.

FOREWORD

IN MANY ways, Ezra Pound has remained the most problematic of modern poets writing in English. Those other major poets whose lives overlapped with his — Yeats, Eliot, Frost, Stevens, even William Carlos Williams, whose work in many respects resembles Pound's — seem by comparison settled into literary history. We sense that their stock will remain more or less constant in value, fade a little with time, perhaps, but remain: and that the readers of poetry will approach their work with some consensus.

Pound is different. For forty years of this century, his reputation was eclipsed. This was not entirely because of his unsavoury political associations, but because of the poetry itself: above all, the *Cantos*. From the beginning of the nineteen-twenties, when Pound left London and committed himself to their writing, the English-speaking academic establishment became increasingly unsure how seriously to regard him. It became normal to think of him as someone who had played a minor role, if only for his Imagism and his encouragement of T S Eliot; but where Eliot rapidly attained academic respectability with his disciplined and intellectually orderly work and his considerable critical abilities, Pound's erratic, ambitious, 'tasteless' and aggressive writings, both poetry and prose, were felt to present horrific formal difficulties and unlimited problems of interpretation. The publication of T S Eliot's edition of *Literary essays of Ezra Pound* in 1954, and of Hugh Kenner's marvellously perceptive *The poetry of Ezra Pound* (1951) were the events which foreshadowed the remarkable upturn in interest in the past two decades. Not that they settled any questions: they catalysed the arguments.

Pound's poetry is now on university syllabuses in many countries besides England and the United States, and Pound scholarship is multilingual; yet students must still struggle with the poetry in the knowledge that critics remain in fundamental disagreement about *how to read* the poetry, how to interpret (especially) the *Cantos*. The aim of this present work is to clarify practice, to question the way in which we go to Pound's work, and our reading strategy. Pound's writing became increasingly allusive and elliptical (his prose as well as his verse) with

7

the passage of time, and we tend to approach it through the identification of sources and references, to try to 'solve' his text as though it were a riddle. One aim of this present work is to question the assumption that Pound's work (or any other modernist poetic text for that matter) responds well to such an approach.

If we assume that the poetry is mimetic, that it represents some kind of 'real life', whether the life and experience of the poet himself, or the reality of his literary tradition stretching from Homer to Joyce, then our reading should indeed involve an identification of the aspects of reality which are mirrored in the poems. Without such identification, we cannot judge the skill, understand the means, or accept the authenticity of the work. We cannot even begin to decide whether the *Cantos* possesses a form, or was merely an anthology of poems, some boring, some great enough to echo forever in the memory. An alternative assumption, of course, is that the mimetic problem comes a poor second to all the questions raised by a reading of the text-in-itself. This in turn raises the theoretical question of the nature of the text. In Pound's case, the body of his writing is so inter-connected that the reader is quickly carried on toward the poet's own theories of structure, especially where they verge on a psychology of reading, or on a view of a relationship between the text and the reader which is focused on the mechanism of Image or ideogram. In either case, the reader is faced with the question of the status and relevance of Pound's prose, or his aesthetic theory. My study is strongly biassed toward a consideration of Pound's aesthetic, for it is clear that the verse and the prose form a surprisingly homogeneous body of writing, despite the informality, carelessness and evasiveness of some of the work.

This book takes Pound's poetry and prose together and examines the evolution of his writing and its aesthetic. That progress was not revolutionary. The adolescent Ezra decided to be a poet, that is of course a Romantic poet. The first section of this work, 'The spirit of Romanticism', is a study of his earliest poetry and prose, up to about 1911. I have examined the contribution of traditional Romantic principles to his development, using as texts both a selection of the early poems, and accompanying prose studies of literary tradition in *The spirit of romance* (1910) and 'I gather the limbs of Osiris' (1911-12). Pound's initial attitudes were highly 'Romantic' in the sense that he accepted an aesthetic, based on Coleridge and Longinus, which emphasised the power of the imagination and the importance of the sublime and ecstatic. This led him both to emphasise the importance to a poet of a power, or energy, in forming and shaping his writing, and the expressive nature of the poetic text. It also led him to approach literary tradition as a treasury of examples of such poetic power — a treasury from which things could be taken and 'made new' for his own day. It

8

is from these aesthetic principles that much of Pound's mature development can be traced.

The second section, 'The Poet as Critic', is an examination of Pound's critical rules and practice, in the attempt to clarify the status of his literary prose. The relationship between Pound's casual prose practices and his theory of the nature of criticism is discussed; and my conclusion is that critical and creative practice are, in Pound's work, deliberately confused. His conceptions of the functions of criticism led Pound toward the cultural and social prose of his later years, and possess important implications for his conception of literary tradition and, especially, his practice of translation. I have made some attempt to distinguish a variety of translation practices in Pound's work, with interesting implications for much of his later poetry. This has led me to question the firmness of a boundary between criticism and creation; and finally to suggest that, given Pound's belief in the very critical function of poetry, the distinctions between prose and poetry vanish in a common function: critic, poet and teacher dissolve into one another, and the reader is left with the writing — limits of genre begin to vanish.

The third section — 'Text and Form' — follows this hint by examining the linguistic basis of Pound's theory of poetry. His old, Romantic notion of the poet's energy alters into a theory of language's energy, and expressionist criteria become linguistic ones. Pound's emphasis moves from the 'sincere' to the 'precise' at about the time of his involvement with Imagisme (1912-14), and his strategy emphasised the reform and modernising of poetic diction. A consequence of this was its answer to the old objections that poetic truth and 'real' truth are at odds. Pound's rejection of Romantic poetry and Romantic diction is enshrined in the poetry from *Ripostes* onward, and in an aesthetic which focuses itself on directness of presentation. The idea of poetry as language led Pound to put forward a theory of the way in which that language is charged with energy and significance, both by the sensual elements of sound and imagery, and the conceptual element which he called 'logopoeia', or verbalism. The real nature of the imagist movement can be questioned; but Pound's own Imagist practice can be seen as the first version of an inclusive aesthetic which evolved, by way of Vorticism and a theory of ideogrammic form, into the fully developed practices of the allusive, elliptical *Cantos*. Both sound and imagery contribute to Imagism; but the most interesting aspect of Pound's aesthetic from this point is the way that it develops into a recognition that the poetic text is a complex of relationships, and that those relationships involve not only the words on the page, but energies which are not in black and white, but which nevertheless control and shape everything. The inevitable conclusion is an approach to a theory of poetry as an event — something which can be understood only by considering the psychology

9

of reading. In this development, Pound's version of Vorticism of course formed a climax.

The fourth section of this book is on 'Knowledge and the *Cantos*'. It builds upon the understanding of Pound's linguistic approach to poetry, with its difficult and tentative development of the concept of logopoeia. In the light of his concept of logopoeia or verbalism, Pound's *Homage to Sextus Propertius* is again approached, and the consequences of logopoeia are traced into techniques of distanciation and inter-textuality, and into a questioning of mimetic principles and authorial intentions. This leads to a question of the nature of truth in a poem, and I have examined the way in which Pound's authorial strategy changes, through a series of the major mature pre-*Cantos* poems from 1914 through 1920, in a way that confirms his rejection of the representational in favour of a linguistic and contextual mode of writing. I have examined 'Near Perigord', *Propertius*, *Hugh Selwyn Mauberley*, and the earliest version of the first *Cantos* in turn, and found the same tendencies, the same implications in all of them. These tendencies are still not confined to verse. The logopoeic literary method which Pound also described as 'ideogrammic' is displayed in his *Guide to Kulchur* (1938), that curious and eclectic prose work which so clearly forms the background to central portions of the *Cantos*. But of course it is the *Cantos* toward which everything tends. In the end, any decision about Pound's work, or status, must depend on our attitude to his major work. I do not claim to have found the meaning of the poem; my argument is in fact that no such claim could be made. However I have ventured to suggest a strategy for starting to read the *Cantos*. It is a strategy, and a theoretical understanding of Pound's project, to which the argument of the whole book has led. I hope that it will be helpful to those who, like me, find endless excitement in the poem.

10

ABBREVIATIONS

REFERENCES to Pound's writings are made, as far as possible, to the most convenient modern edition of his poetry or prose; where relevant, the date of the original publication is also given. The following forms of reference are used:

ABC	*ABC of reading* (London, 1951)
ALS	*A Lume Spento and other early poems* (London, 1965)
Cantos	*The Cantos of Ezra Pound*, rev collected edition (London, 1975) (references shown as Canto number/page number)
CSP	*Collected shorter poems*, 2nd ed (London, 1968)
GB	*Gaudier-Brzeska, a memoir* (London, 1916)
GK	*Guide to Kulchur* (Norfolk, Conn. n d [1952])
Letters	*The letters of Ezra Pound 1907-1941*, edited by D D Paige (London, 1951)
LE	*Literary essays of Ezra Pound*, edited by T S Eliot (London, 1954)
PD	*Pavannes and divisions*, (New York, 1918)
PE	*Polite essays*, (London, 1937)
PM	*Patria mia and the treatise on harmony*, new ed (London, 1962)
SPr	*Selected prose 1909-1965*, edited by William Cookson (London, 1973)
SR	*The spirit of romance*, rev ed (London, 1952)
Translations	*The translations of Ezra Pound* (London, 1953)
(Beinecke)	Unpublished material in the Ezra Pound Archive, Beinecke Rare Book and Manuscript Library, University of Yale
(Paige)	Transcript of letter by/to Pound, made by D D Paige in preparing his edition of *Letters* (above): in Beinecke

I

THE SPIRIT OF ROMANTICISM

Poetry and genius
WHEN Ezra Pound set out, in about 1900, to make himself into a poet, his chosen model was the English late-Romantic Aesthete. For the next ten or twelve years, he followed aesthetic principles which belonged to the mainstream of English nineteenth-century romantic poetry, looking back through Rossetti, Pater, Swinburne and the young Yeats to Wordsworth, Coleridge, and ultimately Longinus. He saw poetry as the poet's song. The world of the poem was the poet's world, his 'phantastikon', created by his image-making poet (SR, 92). For Pound, the poem did not reflect the 'real' world, but rather the experience imaged in the poet's consciousness: 'crescent images of *me*', says the poet in the early poem, 'Plotinus' (ALS, 56). Therefore the young poet wrote, in his essays and poems, about the nature of his own experience and that of his Romantic forefathers. He was not yet much interested in the technical links between experience and its expression: he merely accepted the poet as seer, exile, hero, light of the world.

Pound's aesthetic always seemed rather old-fashioned in its acceptance of an inspiration separate from its expression:

'I knew at fifteen much what I wanted to do. I believed that the "Impulse" is with the gods; that technique is a man's own responsibility. A man either is or is not a great poet, that is not within his control...'[1]

Poetry is an innate capacity; its nature and source are mysterious. Much of Pound's youthful verse expressed wonder at the 'impulse' of poetic genius.

Pound's first three collections of poems – *A Lume Spento* (1908), *A Quinzaine for this Yule* (1908) and *Personae* (1909) – lay great weight on inspiration.[2] Many poems describe the experience of being an artist under the mask, or *persona*, either of one of the English Romantics, or of those Tuscan or Provençal poets in whom Anglo-American writers like Rossetti and Longfellow had been interested. By assuming such a mask, Pound was able to dramatise the mysterious genius out of which a work of art had arisen. The natural form of such a mask lay of course in Pound's imitation of some of the expressive qualities,

13

especially rhythms and cadences, of the original poem in which such genius had been expressed.

What strikes the reader of Pound's earliest poems is that, although the volumes contain many examples of a callow, romantic response to nature, or to imaginary love-affairs, all in the forms and diction of the 'Nineties, there is an unusual degree of emphasis on the sensibility, the search for a romantic sublime, and the specific works of poetic predecessors. If these three volumes possess any single theme, it is the unique and isolated nature of the Artist, and his single-minded self-dedication to art: something like Coleridge's views of the creative imagination is joined to an almost priestly view of the duties which follow upon its possession. There is a portrait of the artist as a social outcast, alienated by his very nature from the world around. The 1908 poem, 'Masks', describes painters, singers, poets and 'wizards', all of them 'magicians', trapped in a material world which isolates and denies them (ALS, 52). Pound probably took his concept of magic from Yeats, whom he much admired, but of course it belongs to that central tradition descending from Coleridge's *Biographia literaria*, Wordsworth's *Prelude*, and Shelley's *Adonais*, whose metaphysical raptures very much resemble Pound's early tone.

To the positive quality of poetic inspiration, Pound added a negative of the alienating materialism in contemporary society, the theme found throughout post-Tennysonian Romanticism. 'In durance' is dated 1907, as though this were an autobiographical account of Pound's unhappiness during his work in Indiana that year, but is actually a very general statement, in Browning's style, of the abyss between all artists and the philistines who surround them:

> ' "These sell our pictures!" Oh well,
> They reach me not, touch me some edge or that,
> But reach me not, and all my life's become
> One flame, that reacheth not beyond
> My heart's own hearth . . .
>   Yea, I am homesick
> After mine own kind that know, and feel
> And have some breath for beauty and the arts.'   (CSP, 34-5)

The pressures of a materialistic society upon the artist assumed the dimensions of an obsession for Pound. Sometimes it is difficult to decide whether such plaints were a reaction to the crassness of America's Gilded Age, which he left in 1908, or simply the usual pose of international Bohemia. However, the effect of the poems like this is to suggest that the true artist glories in the alienation which follows upon his sensibility and dedication, and this is the attitude of a romantic Bohemian, not a literary determinist. The artists of these early poems

14

are in fact all versions of the same aggressive being, for the Singer boasts his own responsiblity for his song: 'Exquisite loneliness:/ Bound of mine own caprice . . .' — 'And lo! I refuse your bidding. / I will not bow to the expectation that ye have.' (ALS, 31-2). (The very lines reject the reader's metrical expectations.) Defiance is the central poetic strategy for the true poet, 'bearer of beauty' on the edges of bourgeois society: 'Though our lips be slain / We see Art vivent and exult to die.' (ALS, 68) Creation is heroic; immortality lies in true Art.

Such isolation is however mitigated by a mysterious spiritual link between the poet and other magus-figures, or the poet and Nature. In these early poems, the artist is an initiate in a mysterious order. References to chthonic Nature, the paganised remains of Romantic Transcendentalism, survive throughout Pound's work and even assume a considerable thematic importance in the *Cantos*. In an explanatory note for 'La Fraisne', a poem so important to Pound that he originally intended it to give its title to his first volume of poetry, Pound attempted to describe the poet's mystical experience thus:

'When the soul is exhausted in fire, then doth the spirit return unto its primal nature . . .'
. . .
'Being freed of the weight of a soul "capable of salvation or damnation," a grievous striving thing that after much straining was mercifully taken from me; . . . leaving me thus *simplex naturae*, even so at peace and trans-sentient as a wood pool I made it.' (ALS, 14)

'It' — the poem — is a mask-exploration of mood and personality from one of the mediaeval romances which fascinated Pound; what he is claiming is that the poem 'comes' *through* the poet, like the breath of inspiration from an unknown muse.

In 'The flame', Pound was more explicit: the poet can 'pass through' the 'net of days and hours', leaving behind his bodily identity which is the accidental 'mirror' or temporal reality, to merge with a panpsychic soul (CSP, 64-5).[3] It is this kind of statement that has led critics to comment on the passivity of the poetic experience which is described in these early years, as opposed to an energetic, form-making imagination which becomes central to Vorticist theory five years later. Perhaps the central distinction to be made is between Pound's focus during this early period, when he was writing of the dream of artistic sensibility, and that of 1914 or 1915, when the emphasis was on the poem as language. Now, for example in 'Salve O Pontifex!', Pound was addressing the poet as a Bacchic high priest, maddened by divine afflatus, prophesying in obscure, tangled verses (ALS, 63-8). Elements of initiation, possession, and ecstasy, and the reference to Eleusinian rites, point not only to the nature of a young poet's derivative ideas, but to elements

15

of a myth which Pound soon reinforced by his discovery of the *trobar clus* tradition of Provençal poetry. In his *Sonnets and ballatte of Guido Cavalcanti* (1912), Pound argued for the existence of a tradition of secretive, deliberately-obscure poetry whose inner meaning could be understood only by the initiate. He continued to use this idea through the *Cantos*; a section of Canto 79 powerfully presents the kind of experience which is merely postulated in the early poems:

> 'Here are lynxes   Here are lynxes
> Is there a sound in the forest
>   of pard or of bassarid
> or crotale   or of leaves moving?'

>   'Cythera, here are lynxes
> Will the scrub-oak burst into flower?
> There is a rose vine in this underbrush
> Red? white? No, but a colour between them
>   When the pomegranate is open and the light falls
> half thru it'

(Cantos, 79/490)

This is experience itself, rising to the divine vision at the culmination of the canto: the goddess Aphrodite and the light of Helios.

But as well as their shared relationship with the natural world, Pound's poets join in a community with fellow-artists living and dead:

> 'Aye, I am wistful for my kin of the spirit
> And have none about me save in the shadows
> Whence come *they*, surging of power, 'DAEMON',
> "Quasi KALOUN," S.T. says Beauty is most
>   that, a 'calling to the soul.'
> Well then, so call they, the swirlers out of the mist of
>   my soul,
> They that come mewards bearing old magic.'

(CSP, 34)

Longinus, whose treatise *On the sublime* Pound's work constantly echoes, saw poetic inspiration as the product of the communion between the soul of the living poet and those masters of the past: a spiritual tradition. Daemons were spirits of passion associated with Platonic intuitive Beauty, and the quotation from Coleridge refers us to his essay 'On the principles of genial criticism':

'The Beautiful arises from the perceived harmony of an object, whether sight or sound with the inborn and constructive rules of judgement and imagination: and it is always intuitive. . . . Hence the Greeks called a beautiful object *kalon quasi kaloun*; ie *calling on* the soul, which receives instantly, and welcomes it as something connatural.'[4]

16

Pound's interpretation is that beauty, which he associated with the emotional rather than the conceptual, is intuitively perceived; and that the form assumed by beauty is of the 'old magic' of tradition. In several poems he toyed with the idea that inspiration is a kind of possession, not by muse or god but by the spirits of great poets and prophets of the past expressing themselves through him:[5]

> '. . . the souls of all men great
> At times pass through us,
> And we are melted into them, and are not
> Save as reflexions of their souls.'   (ALS, 108)

These early poems refer repeatedly to the poet's sacrifice of identity to his work, for 'the thing that matters is the great art' rather than its creator.[6] At this point it seems that the expressionist theory of poetry — the idea that the poem is the direct personal expression of its author's thoughts and experience — has been strangely diverted to a concept of the communal, unindividualised nature of the poetic mind: the poet's ego is subsumed in the unconscious of a poetic tradition. This identification is a curious romantic by-path which leads eventually to the centre of Pound's modernist techniques.

By 1909, Pound's poems had expressed a series of assumptions belonging to a very broad complex of Romanticism: that a poet possesses unusual emotional power and perceptivity, that the poem expresses his emotional being, that the function of poetry is to appeal to the readers' intuitive perceptions of the 'calling' of beauty. With minor exceptions, Pound was more concerned with the nature of the poet — of himself — than of the poem. In 1909 he had scarcely begun his study of the craft of writing, and his few statements about technique were cursory and contradictory. The words he applied to poetry were conventional romantic metaphors: dreams, song, harmonies, beauties, jewels, flame — the imagery of English Aestheticism or the 'Genteel tradition' of American romanticism

Even his prose work was unanalytical and all but avoided any reference to the actual mode of expression. Several of Pound's early short essays published in a Philadelphia monthly review set out to provide some kind of critical comment, but beyond giving prose paraphrases of certain poems, the writing does not really engage with the poetry which is its subject-matter. The essays are in fact Pound's celebrations of the Romance of History and of artistic Beauty. They are the work, not of a craftsman or even a formalist critic, but of an old-fashioned *belles-lettriste* with a time-traveller's passion for antiquity. In a very similar way, the pseudonymous preface to Pound's second collection, *A Quinzaine for this Yule* (1908), meditated on the wonder of an aesthetic experience:

17

'Beauty should never be presented explained. It is Marvel and Wonder, . . . and . . . a slow understanding (slow even though it be a succession of lightning understandings and perceptions) as of a figure in a mist . . . ' (ALS, 87)

Pound owed these lightning understandings to his reading of Longinus.[8] His clumsy justification of obscurity, and his suggestion that the work incarnates ideal beauty, are consistent with statements in the poems of the collection. And the problem of defining that misty figure is given, as in his mature critical theory,[9] to the reader rather than the poet; and here, again, only the poet and his self-expression were actually under consideration.

Many of the poems which accompanied this prose introduction deal with the metamorphic moment, that moment of lightning understanding or intuitive perception:

> 'The light became her grace and dwelt among
> Blind eyes and shadows that are formed as men;
> Lo, how the light doth melt us into song . . . '   (CSP, 52)

> 'I stood still and was a tree amid the wood,
> Knowing the truth of things unseen before . . . '   (CSP, 17)

> 'I catch the character I happen to be interested in at the
> . . . moment of song, self-analysis, or sudden understanding
> or revelation.'   (Letters, 36)

Again Pound's focus is on experience; and again — now in the Longinian instant of illumination — his earliest theory contains the seeds of Pound's modernism.

On virtue

When Pound decided to write up the lectures he had been giving in London during 1909 and 1910 and publish them as a book, *The spirit of romance*, these aesthetic 'feelings' had not really prepared him for the task of not merely perceiving the existence of emotional intensity in poetry, but identifying and analysing its sources, and also suggesting the nature of the necessary relationship between the poetic feeling and its mode of expression. He had developed certain attitudes which can be traced to his reading of Longinus, Dante, Coleridge and Walter Pater.[10] His conception of the imagination, the esemplastic power, as the foundation of poetry belongs to the tradition of Coleridge, but from Dante he had learned the possibility of discovering a 're-usable' literary tradition — that is, a tradition of poetry representing the best of past work which a modern author could use in learning his own trade. Longinus perhaps appealed most to Pound's youthful emotionalism. The idea of sublimity permeates Pound's writings, often in the form of a concern for its emotional product, ecstasy. Ecstasy is a word which haunts Pound's early writings. This, with his distinction between the mysterious and magical poetic impulse and its visible means of expression, and also his belief in the anarchic genius of the artist — all belong to Longinus and the Longinian tradition in England.

Pound struggled to write *The spirit of romance* during the winter of 1909-1910, at the end of his first year in London. The book surveys Romance literatures of the Middle Ages; a large proportion of its text consists of listings of authors, some selection from their work — usually no more than a taste in a few lines or stanzas — and a little information about the authors' historical importance. In the preface, Pound claimed to analyse qualities 'which were potent in the mediaeval literature of the Latin tongues, and are, I believe, still potent in our own.' (SR, 7) The attitude, which is premised on the idea of a living literary tradition with technical continuity, is interesting; but the purpose of the book is not clearly realised, and its critical method is inadequate for that purpose. The chapter on 'The quality of Lope de Vega' is a case in point. It consists essentially of a list of plays with elementary plot summaries, and translations of some passages — translations which paraphrase the work but establish no linguistic distinction. The synopses are brief — too brief to demonstrate structural qualities divorced from the linguistic. Ironically, the chapter remains one of the vaguest and most uncertain in the book, given that Pound had intended to make Lope the subject of postgraduate research and presumably had a special knowledge of the work. Pound all but acknowledged his own defeat: 'No formula of criticism is . . . of any great use in trying to define him. He is not a man, he is a literature.' (SR, 207) This is a failure of critical practice, but it is based on an inadequate understanding of critical theory. Such a failure is not universal. The chapter on Camoens is more satisfactory descriptive criticism, and led Pound to successful evaluation:

'The further narrative . . . is beautiful and full of music; but it is the beauty of words and cadences, and of expression, . . . that subtle understanding which is genius and the dayspring of the arts. How wise is De Quincey, when he speaks of the "miracle which can be wrought simply by one man's feeling a thing more keenly, understanding it more deeply, than it has ever been felt before." In this pass fails Camoens...' (SR, 219)

This sweeping judgement still depends on Pound's naive conception of poetic genius; but having in this case freed himself from the wonder of that genius, he has become capable of making certain detailed textual evaluations. However in this chapter, as in the other, Pound remains unwilling to undertake extended analysis of qualities of the expression. If Pound's critical theorising, like that of T S Eliot, is often seen as

19

foreshadowing the work of the New Critics, it is true that neither here, nor in most of his later work, was Pound able to undertake the kind of practical textual analysis which was really called for by an expressionist theory, and which is associated with formalist criticism of the mid-century. Pound's critical practice, in *The spirit of romance* as in most of his literary reviewing throughout his career, is the summary judgement of the intellectual and emotional range of an author. His belief in Lope's genius leaves further comment abstracted, and in the long run Pound can *assert* the existence of masterpieces, heroes, joys, ecstasies, as he fails to *demonstrate* any consistent 'spirit' of romance (SE, 7-8).

And yet his critical practice here seems appropriate to the context of the book and its romantic emphasis. Pound wanted to discriminate the emotional power of poetry. Believing in the poet's special creative genius, he looked for some power existing separate from the discourse which expressed it: an ideal force which existed *before* it had formed the poem. Biographical anecdotes[11] remind us that Pound saw himself in the role of the Romantic Poet, all pose and passion, and he had an emotional investment in the doctrines of innate genius, inspiration and enthusiasm. His prose writing at this stage was part hack-work, part an alternative expression of faith in the emotional superiority of the artist and the emotional equation of the poem. What is lacking in *The spirit of romance* is an understanding of the creative imagination whose workings could be analysed rather than merely felt. He approached such a concept in the single case of Dante, in whose work he had begun to trace an intensity which held together isolated mediaeval qualities (SR, 167). He made an attempt to demonstrate the form of this poetic cohesiveness by comparing Shakespearean imagery with Dante's, and by discussing Dante's metaphors (SR, 158-9). The passage is the most lively and most successful of the book, and interestingly follows shortly on a passage in which he had confessed a sense of inadequacy, realising the extent to which his criticism had become merely a statement of faith (SR, 154). The concern with metaphor as an expression of poetic energy is a key to the next development of his poetic.

Pound needed some clearer understanding of what he felt about the poetic sensibility; he needed to develop it as a theory of the creative imagination which would account for some of the effects of the poem on the reader. He did not achieve this in *The spirit of romance*; but it is developed in the series of essays which Pound wrote to continue that work and published under the title 'I gather the limbs of Osiris' in A R Orage's weekly, *The new age*, in the following winter of 1911-1912. In these Pound announced a new discovery, a quality which he calls *virtù*: a force or creative energy emanating from the poet's creative mind which lends uniqueness and intensity to the aesthetic object. This is the power which caused the 'crystallisation' he had perceived in

20

Dante's work; and in the sixth essay of the series, 'On virtue' (SPr, 28-31), he identified it with 'soul' and with a 'continuous under-current' of emotion which he perceived in great poetry. For Pound, the poet's true priorities are clear: first he must perceive the nature of his own *virtù*, his uniqueness; then he must express it; finally he should study techniques in order to develop his means of expressing it. In the uniqueness of vision and consistency of identity, he found a sense of organic completeness in the work of great authors — Homer, Dante, Chaucer, Shakespeare. Such authors, Pound tells us, create their own microcosms; and at this point he returned to the perceived uniqueness of that microcosm, rather than its mode of expression, as the touchstone of genius.

Despite the Italian form, Pound undoubtedly derived his *virtù* from Walter Pater's preface to *The Renaissance*, a book which had much influenced his thinking and probably the very concept of *The spirit of romance*. Pater had written that 'virtue' is the motive power in 'what the heat . . . of imagination has wholly fused and transformed'.[12] Virtue appears to be another name for Coleridge's secondary imagination; Pater was writing in terms of a genius which overtops its age, taking as an example the 'unique, incommunicable faculty' which is the virtue or 'active principle' in his work. (For Pater, this virtue resides largely in Wordsworth's imagery; Pound, describing the Image a couple of years later, went to the *Prelude* for one of his major examples.) Pater's own aim was to defend an impressionistic criticism which answers subjectively to such a force. Pound's concerns were somewhat different, for he was bringing his various sources together to form an idea of the imagination 'conceiving' rather than merely reflecting reality, and therefore acting creatively rather than mimetically. But he adopted Pater's affective concerns; and it is through 'virtue' and its implications that the direction of his earliest criticism can best be understood.

First, the concept casts considerable light on the purposes of the *personae* poems. When, at the beginning of a poem like 'Sestina: Altaforte'. Pound would write: 'Judge ye! Have I dug him up again?' (CSP, 42) he was implying that the aim of such a poem was to reproduce the *virtù* of the *persona* of the poet, Bertran de Born. Where, as in this case, the subject is a historical person, and specifically a poet, Pound had the document of *virtù* (the original text) to work with. The composition of a poem like this was therefore a *critical activity*, in that it involved a large degree of precise analytical awareness as well as the ability to express that perception.

Second, Pound's development of the idea of *virtù* goes far to explain the nature of the changing emphasis in his early poetic. The uncertainties of *The spirit of romance* are a consequence of attempting to identify an imaginative quality without having defined it, by means of selective quotations stiffly translated into an inadequate literary English. A repeated misquotation of Coleridge reveals Pound's bias in this book: 'Our genuine admiration of a great poet is for a continuous undercurrent of feeling; it is everywhere present but seldom anywhere as a separate excitement.' In fact Coleridge wrote: 'Our genuine admiration of a great poet is a continuous undercurrent of feeling . . .'[13] Pound had misread a statement about response as one about the poetic nature, in line with his own contemporary concern for genius rather than for a scholarly or critical competence. Coleridge's sentence is just acceptable as autobiographical confession; Pound's version epitomises his unwillingness to move away from his fascination with genius, to criteria of expression. This might be expected in a thinking which was so heavily Longinian. Yet the problems of a continuous-undercurrent theory of the kind which Pound was supporting with the false authority of Coleridge make criticism impossible, for it is logically impossible to demonstrate a continuous undercurrent by any normal process of critical practice.

Pound is left asserting his articles of faith; but in stumbling recognition of the awkward corner into which his faith has led him, he also offers a further, inconsistent, Longinian principle: 'Another test of the poetic art is the single line.' Yet the 'single line is, it is true, an insufficient text of a man's art, but it is a perfect test of his natural vigor and of his poetic nature.' (SR, 50, 110) The second thought is almost worse than the first. However, Pater also taught Pound that the critic's task is to 'trace that active principle, to disengage it, to mark the degree in which it penetrates his verse',[14] and Pound was trying to do this without the self-discipline of connected analytical discourse, which he was finding difficult or impossible to write.[15] *The spirit of romance* demonstrates that touchstone quotations and attempts to reproduce the Longinian thunderbolt effect were inadequate means of revealing pervasive imaginative qualities. Only occasionally, as in discussions of Dante and of the Provençal poets, did Pound begin to link the pervasiveness of inspiration with the techniques of expression. The conception of *The spirit of romance* is based on emotion as a creative and formal energy; but although Pound repeatedly asserted the presence of this power, in the effect of sublimity, he could not account for his perception so long as quotation was his only device to support it. It was only his idea of *virtù* that gave him a word for the energy he had dimly perceived, and allowed his work to develop from the nineteenth-century impressionistic by-way into which he had gone; and in the 'Osiris' essays he set out to remedy his failure by presenting serious translations of whole poems into forms which reflected the discourse of the originals.

The theory of the essential energy of poetic sensibility formed the

22

basis for Pound's mature poetic. It is the basis for understanding Pound's version of Imagism; strengthened further, *virtù* became the 'fluid force [directed] against circumstance'. the pattern-forming agency of Vorticism.[15] By this means, the secondary imagination of Romantic theory — as opposed to the observing, reflecting faculty — became the linch-pin of Pound's most belligerently 'modern' theories. His later work is never consistently free of a tendency to distinguish between the poem as expression, and some 'residue of perception', or unexpressed energy, which he saw as a kind of *physical* force tending toward the creation of form, or with a potential for expression (LE, 151, 154). This early respect for *virtù* left Pound with a belief that even in the energy of merely latent forms there is greatness. As his ideas assumed a more moralistic tone during the 1920s and 1930s, Pound tended to confuse aesthetic with moral effects, and what he called '*directio voluntatis*', the moral guidance of Will, joined the intellectual and emotional aspects of poetic energy. This attitude haunts the *Cantos*, from the 'Malatesta' sequence to *Thrones*.[16] Here, literary theory passes into the realm of cultural values and ideology. But although the respect for intensity or energy itself led Pound to ends which seem far from his Romantic beginnings, those ends were always inherent in his ideas. Perhaps Pound expressed them most strangely in suggesting that the Italian poet, Gabriele d'Annunzio, was able to 'speak with more authority' than other poets because during the First World War he had been involved in the capture of Trieste (LE, 192). Here is the ultimate slippage from poem to author, but the slide was implicit as well as explicit in most of Pound's criticism.

In *The spirit of romance* it is explicit. Pound's critical method is to name poets, to write of their work generally as a homogeneity which expresses the author's meaning and intention. Yet his theory was not quite consistent with this practice. Writing of Romance literatures in terms of a tradition stretching back to early mediaeval Latin writings, Pound described poetry as a 'sort of inspired mathematics, which gives us equations, not for abstract figures . . . but . . . for the human emotions.' (SR, 14) To see a poem as an equation implies a middle term which is open to attention and consideration; it suggests a shift of attention from the inexplicable impulse to the explicable mode. The methodological difference between *The spirit of romance* and its sequel, the 'Osiris' essays, is that the latter begin to engage seriously with poetry as texts. The essay series begins with the translation of 'The seafarer' into a modern English which retains much of the sounds and rhythmical patterns of the original; translations from the Provençal similarly reflect the forms of the originals. What is happening here is that Pound has begun to see his task in terms of texts and techniques; virtue, or *virtù*, is discussed in a technical context, an essay 'On technique' presents energy in terms of a lasting and effective literary tradition; and the more theoretical passages of writing are interspersed (especially in the central discussion of Arnaut Daniel) with examples of his rhyme schemes, formal problems, and poetic diction (eg SPr, 29-30). Pound is now seeing the poem as an objective rhetorical text and finding means of evaluation which are not impressionistic but linguistic and analytical. In his fourth and fifth collections of verse — *Exultations* (1909) and *Canzoni* (1911) — there is less interest in the exploration of the subjective state through the presentation of *personae* than in experiments with diction and metre. With the wisdom of hindsight, we can see how they prepare for the Imagist breakthrough (although they do not foretell its nature) in their concern for the textual devices which are that middle element of the expressive poetic equation.

This change of direction was anticipated in the 'Osiris' essays when Pound settled his interest on what he called 'donative' artists: those whose creative-critical discriminations allow them to donate a *new* literary quality to the body of tradition of which their poems form a part. The donation was variously seen: at first, in fact, Pound thought it might be the inexplicable virtue, or state of consciousness (S Pr, 25, 29-30). However, the idea of the poem as an equation for the emotions implies an essential precision: the statement $2 + 2 = 17$ is probably invalid. Therefore, if poetry is a 'verbal statement of emotional values', it must follow that it 'aims at giving a feeling precisely evaluated'.[17] If the logic of this did not wholly enter Pound's theory all at once, at least the discovery of a need for exactness began to modify the obscurantism of his earlier feelings for the poet-priest, as he discovered that 'technique is the means of conveying an exact impression of exactly what one means in such a way as to exhilarate'. (SPr, 33) In other words, the poetic content is a complex of concept and emotion which has been encoded in language of the most appropriate kind. Furthermore, what is signified in this language is not just the poet's experience, in accordance with the old expressive concept, but something which is being transferred to the reader in such a way as to affect him strongly and pleasantly. In his interest in affect there is the kernel of a notion of transference which is important to an understanding of both the Image and the ideogrammic theory.

Perhaps the single most important key to Pound's early work and the poetic behind it is the concept of *virtù* or energy. It is noticeable that Pound's interest was not in a poetry of representation, except in the special sense of a poetry which presents the poet's experience of the physical universe. His admiration for a Dante or a Villon lay not in the precision with which a mirror is held up to nature, but rather in the nature of the mirror itself, the 'great sub-surge of his truth and his sincerity' (SR, 163), which provides the interpretative function of art.

24

He was not yet ready to lay his great emphasis on precision of technique, but he saw 'hyper-scientific precision' as a 'touchstone and assay of the artist's authenticity'. (SR, 87) In this context, values of sincerity and authenticity denote a poetic theory which is still firmly poet-centred and in which truth is based on the authority of the poet. At the same time, they imply the beginning of a search for a guarantee of that truthfulness.

Tradition and the individual poet
If the primary poetic motive lay, for Pound at least, in the individual *virtù*, the second was to be found in a literary tradition: and not merely in that hazy glamour of the brotherhood of poets, but in the body of practice — training, craftsmanship — which gradually grew to assume in his thinking the status of a cultural heritage. Above all, this was a *usable* tradition. It consists of aesthetic objects, documents, texts which are the treasury of technical continuities as well as the individual's *virtù*.

Of the one hundred and eighty poems which Pound chose to reprint in his definitive edition of *Personae: the collected poems of Ezra Pound* (1926), few are a simple subjective record. The forty-two taken from pre-1912 volumes almost all allude to literary matters. Nearly half are translations or imitations of poets from Yeats to Propertius. Fourteen 'mask' poems reproduce some quality which Pound had discovered in the work of another poet, either by stylistic imitations or direct reference. Even poems like 'The flame' and 'In durance', which are apparently simple records of his own experience, comment generally on the artist's experience of the world (CSP, 64-5, 34-5); furthermore, they are so pervasively influenced by recognisable predecessors, especially Browning, that although they neither allude specifically to a literary tradition nor even assert its existence, many seem to express insights into a literary tone or historical quality which Pound, and now his readers, associated especially with the Provençal and English late-Romantic material. Even when we come to the aggressively colloquial modernity of the poems from *Ripostes* (1912) and *Lustra* (1916), we are in the context of Roman satire, and of the attempt to 'translate' Fenollosa's versions of Chinese into English twentieth-century verse.

The same pervasive concern with a tradition marks Pound's prose. Those elegant essays which the young Ezra published in a Philadelphia periodical, *Book news monthly*, between 1906 and 1909, were no more than overblown records of his marvelling discovery of the glamour and pastness of the past.[18] But when he came to *The spirit of romance* the focus was beginning to sharpen, as the Dante chapter most clearly shows. Although neither his own translations nor the Rossetti translations which he used adequately show it,[19] what is hovering behind this writing

25

is a belief that a broad but detailed knowledge of the materials of tradition provides a corrective for both shallowness of vision and inadequate technique. The preface to the book acknowledges the existence of a literary tradition in which all authors and all writings exist, in a sense, contemporaneously — on an equal footing, equally to be studied, understood and used (SR, 7-8). This is the perception of a young poet. It becomes clearer in the 'Osiris' essays; in fact, the desire to study the usable tradition is the motive for their composition, and not only for discussions of the nature of poets and poems, but for translations like 'The seafarer' in which the words and verse-forms of the original are mirrored.

The assumption which precedes the preface to *The spirit of romance*, as well as the 'Osiris' enterprise, is that literature forms an organic tradition, a body whose parts are actively related. Pound therefore discussed literature as a body containing forces of regeneration and also *symptomatic* elements, or texts, which logically implies the existence of other elements in relation to which they are paradigmatic. Given this model, literary scholarship must take an overview of the body of art. The scholar-critic becomes a gardener, tending the living and fruitful branches of the art and pruning back those which are weak or dead. In the second 'Osiris' essay Pound described a new method of scholarship, the selection and comparison of what he called 'luminous' or 'interpretive' details (SPr, 21-4).[20] Irrationally, his argument boths suggests the organic relationship of the elements in the tradition, and implies that they are separable, that some of them can be isolated as illuminating, interpreting or implying the whole. Pound had developed a metacritical equivalent of his equally ambivalent theory of evaluation, stated in *The spirit of romance* when he simultaneously argued the 'continuous undercurrent' theory and his belief in the value of evaluative touchstones.

The conception of an organic tradition has a consequence for critical practice. The genetic code of a living organism can be determined by analysis of a tiny proportion; thus Pound's idea that the traditional is both organic and re-usable means that a *functional* understanding of a few typical or symptomatic works can lead to the intellectual and thence artistic control of the whole — in other words, to the ability to create a new master-work.

Yet Pound's theory is simultaneously organic and hierarchical. When he categorised poets as inventors, masters, and diluters of tradition (LE, 23), he was developing a hierarchical view of poets beginning with Homer, the primitive inventor whom Pound saw as lacking the education of a preceding tradition, but whose *virtù* or emotional control was more than enough compensation; masters like Shakespeare or Chaucer whose special expressive genius surpasses the limited working tradition on

26

which they could draw; and poets of lesser *virtù* who need to learn an independent critical judgement and expressive skill through comparative studies in the available literary tradition (LE, 23). For these last, their practical limitation is in their *techne*, or learned theory and training; this is why the most important literary criticism is a study performed both by and for the poet.

The addition of a rather neo-classical idea of 're-usable' tradition to his earliest Romanticism is typical of the accretive methods of Pound's thought. A practice which focuses on the relationship between poet and poem will be based on the assumptions that the source of the text lies in the author's experience, and that the text reflects that experience. For Pound, however, that experience was always in some sense the experience of other poets' experience: this is the weight of his idea which was clearly expressed in something like 'Masks' (ALS, 52) and in the *persona* poems. The notion of the brotherhood of artists, however, opens the way for a traditionalism in which poets are classified as inventors, masters and followers, and literature itself is seen in terms of discovery, mastery, and imitations of greater or lesser value and skilfulness. In later concepts of *virtù*, energy and will, there are personal factors still beneath all the concrete, universal and re-usable elements of the craft, but they remain essentially inexplicable. It was only the aspects of practice which traditionalism could understand and classify (LE, 10-12, *passim*). Therefore his critical theory and practice turned rapidly to a concern with modes of expression, although mingled with technically-oriented statements of all kinds can be found dogmatic assertions of the unanalysable powers of the creative individual, and a lurking myth of great, original, creative heroes. It is this romantic hero-worship which ultimately shapes the thematic materials of Pound's poetry, the whole poetic endeavour of the *Cantos* and, as we shall see, most of the related critical endeavour of post-Imagiste theory.

The special technical concerns of the critic-poet dominated the 'Osiris' essays and Pound's immediate interests for the next six or seven years. After *The spirit of romance* there is less of the celebration of the pastness of the past, for Pound was no longer writing as the teacher to the general student: his context is the poet's rather than the literary historian's. Now Pound rejected the work of describing historical documents in their context, throwing out the occasional disdainful reference to the 'washing-lists' of the academic scholar collecting 'irrelevant' details and dealing only in the accepted literary canon. For the poet, all literature is a-historically significant; it is contemporaneous in a way which outrages the historian's exactitudes. 'It is the mark of the artist that he, and he almost alone, is indifferent to oldness or newness.' (LE, 280) The poet-critic focuses upon the donative in the tradition — poems which are in some way a special contribution of either technique

27

or mode of perception, something which provides both a touchstone for self-evaluation, and a method which can be re-used by the modern writer. Because of his organic and a-chronological model, Pound concluded that a poet could literally waste his time in repeating work already done: a curious view which takes the organic and communal nature of writing to an extreme. It led him to formulate ideas about the critical education of the young poet by a comparative study and evaluation of all writings, involving the elimination of repetitions and the ordering of literary knowledge for re-use (LE, 75). In the 1913 essay, 'The tradition', which is concerned specifically with a tradition of methods of relating sound and meaning in verse, Pound identified a concept of rhythm through examples taken from Greek and Provençal work, related it to English examples, then used the comparison to educe a general rule for poetic composition 'to the cadence, as . . . all good poets . . .' (LE, 93). In other words, he was seeking to give a universal and objectively-perceived validity to free verse by writing an essay which claims to be a 'first-hand untrammeled, unprejudiced examination of the finest possible examples of all those sorts of verse'. (LE, 93) The essay is an excellent example of his traditionalist strategy.

From the concept of *virtù* there came, as Pound turned openly to questions of technique, the proposal that language expresses emotional energies by means of the sound, imagery and tone of the words. From his desire to master such verbal qualities, Pound took the logical step of asserting the existence of a whole range of verbal techniques visible in their contexts within literary tradition and available, like an artist's palette of colours, as pure qualities or techniques available to the educated poet (LE, 215-7). Given such a strategy, the purity and intensity of the relevant 'colour' or literary mode becomes more practically important than either the whole *form* of the work in which the quality is found, or the cognitive content of the work. Poetry, in short, comes to be seen as a rich and variable thesaurus, full of technical touchstones.

This is why Pound's traditionalistic criticism turned to the drawing up of guides to reading, guides to a tradition seen in terms of a palette of qualities: in short, a curriculum for the study of the art of writing. He developed the first of his guides in a series of letters written in 1916 to Iris Barry (Letters, 137-43); it became a reading list of recommendations for wider and wider audiences of literary students, reaching a culmination in *How to read* (1929), and a final expansion in the critical anthology, *ABC of reading* (1934), where theory, technical comment, and exemplary poetic texts join as the logical outcome of the strategy.

What *was* Pound's tradition, his 'KOMPLEAT KULTURE' (LE, 137)? In 1916 it resembled the course of a study which he himself had followed as a university student, even to a recommendation that Barry should read J W Mackail's survey, *Latin literature*, a book which had certainly influenced Pound's youth and probably even the conception of *The spirit of romance*, although he no longer trusted its judgements. He divided his list of material confusingly into items seen as models for the specialised expressive attainment of the young poet, and examples of 'great' literature which should be read in order to develop a general historical awareness. The second purpose is justification for including the kind of translation which he had used in *The spirit of romance* although it could not teach the monoglot reader anything about the forms of the original; and in one confusing instance, he recommends a prose translation of that very Greek verse which he is presenting as a 'storehouse' of poetic rhythms. To some extent, such confusions invalidate the argument — unless we regard the communication as confessional, telling us that Pound had discovered in the cadences of Propertius, in the hardness of Villon, certain technical modes which he himself was trying to re-use. Warnings against the luxuriance of Swinburne's Villon translation, or the style of the Provençal poets, Cavalcanti, or Dante, can only be understood in terms of his consciousness of a personal struggle to modernise the late-Romantic diction of his early poetry: 'Very possibly ALL this mediaeval stuff is very bad for one's style.' (Letters, 138) Because the tradition must be *usable* in this sense, he omits most English verse: not so much because he had revised his early evaluation of Chaucer and Shakespeare, as because such poets had proved too seductive for the apprentice who was his own younger self, or for anyone unaware of the need to take such writers with that grain of critical salt to be found in the properly self-conscious study of them which is involved in a radical imitation of such overwhelming models.[21] The English element was restored to the canon of greatness in *ABC of reading*, but the audience for this later work had expanded to general students of literature, whose needs were less restricted to a poet's strategy.

Once again: the peculiarities and inconsistencies of Pound's traditionalism can *only* be understood in terms of his primary concern as a poet, with the writing of poetry. Although in his earliest work he had been the archaiser, delving into the past for its colour, its romantic remoteness, now his attitude has become limited to the writer's purpose. His emphasis is on invention, on naming of authors who provide something new in the treasury. His 1916 *caveat* to Barry applies more or less to his later curricular provisions:

'One has got constantly to be thinking that "this is fine, but this is not really the right way to do it". Your first job is to get the tools for your work. Later on you can stuff yourself up with erudition . . .' (Letters, 140)

The peculiar omissions are a product of this purpose. In the essay 'On criticism in general' (1923), Pound broke off his list of poets abruptly with Villon, asserting that for centuries after that poetry was merely rhetorical ornamentation; now he will reject even Shakespeare because technically his work contains 'nothing that isn't replaceable by something else . . .'[22] He make the assertion without demonstration or support: Pound's version of history is based on a specific and normative version of historical inventiveness, combined with a criterion of directness in the presentation of content. For the same kind of reason, French novelists — Stendhal, Balzac, Flaubert — are included because Pound held that in the nineteenth century the only respectable writing style was found in French prose.

What Pound's version of tradition ignores is both the conceptual content and the genre or structure of literary works. It functions almost entirely on the level of language, or textuality, and the criterion of value is a conception of verbal precision, the *mot juste*, which in his writings seems to be divorced from social or historical contextualisation and presented as an abstract linguistic principle. Once again, there is the extraordinarily a-historical quality of Pound's historical tradition. The weight of his theory is directed not at the past, but the present, at function and purpose. If, as Pound claimed, 'the only way one can learn is by observing the changes necessary if one is to have a corresponding quality in changed conditions',[23] and if he advises the reader that it is always best to know the *oldest* poem of a given kind (ABC, 47), or if he suggests that the aim of reading is to grasp the full nature of the palette of literature and that a very limited number of examples of a pure type will suffice for this, then what he is actually saying is that there is a distinction between reading for enjoyment, and reading for the purpose of making critical discriminations of technical inventiveness. The specific demands of the usable predominate. And tradition can be seen for what it is: synchronic, linguistic, practical.

The criterion of usefulness, which Pound developed through his curricula and in much of his critical writing about past literatures, illuminates a progression in his poetry from the romantic enjoyment of the past to its renewal in the handling of historical documents. By translation and adaptation or imitation, or by quoting portions of a text in the reviving context of the modern poem, Pound 'makes-new', or recontextualises it, for the twentieth century. 'Experiment aims at writing that will have a relation to the present analogous to the relation which past masterwork had to the life of its time.'[23] The *Cantos*, described by Pound as a poem which includes history, is in this sense a tradition; but so is most of Pound's work. The intertextuality of poetry is strongly suggested by traditionalist theory; it was Pound's deliberate

30

purpose to write poetry consciously, firmly, in the context of other poems preceding it.

Pound's traditionalism ultimately reveals a phenomenological approach to literature. This is clearest in his *Guide to Kulchur* (1938), the penultimate version of the 'kompleat kulture' foreseen over twenty years before. (The incomplete *Cantos*, naturally, is the final version.) In *Kulchur*, Pound took all human history as the material for a new *'paideuma'*, and from it sought to trace the significant elements to shape a new learning. The *paideuma* is defined in terms of an individual's experience of the world.[24] Historical details are treated achronologically, like documents in the literary tradition:

'We do NOT know the past in chronological sequence. It may be convenient to lay it out . . . with dates pasted on here and there, but what we know we know by ripples and spirals eddying out from us and from our time.' (GL, 60)

Pound's version of history, like literary history, is usable in that it is known by individual experience. It is not in the end the objective fact or the physical construct which has primacy, but the grasp of the fact of the thing, the way in which the intellectual and emotional experience of the fact by the individual forms a new complex of significant meaning.[25] The consequences are clear. The history which is encapsulated in the *paideuma*, or the literary history in the tradition which is a usable tradition, exists in the words of the text and is only to be grasped by the reader in terms of the text itself.

II

THE POET AS CRITIC

The practice of criticism
THE usual reader, turning to standard modern texts like Pound's
Collected shorter poems or the recent collected *Cantos*, and supplement-
ing them with *Literary essays of Ezra Pound*, may only gradually become aware of the problems of the status of his prose. We tend to think
of the literary criticism of a poet like Coleridge, Arnold or Eliot in
terms of the weakening of poetic impulse in someone never very prolific.
Pound, conversely, wrote immense quantities of prose material during
his entire literary career. The standard bibliography[1] lists thirty-two
assorted prose books and pamphlets (not including translated works),
a number of books and pamphlets including prose contributions, and
somewhere between seventeen and eighteen hundred contributions to
periodicals which of course included some brief notes and letters
to the editor, as well as the more considerable book, art and music
reviews and major or minor literary and political essays, which is an
average of over thirty per year for fifty-six years, excluding translations.
Pound was also a prolific letter-writer; and many letters are of much
more than biographical interest, as D D Paige's edition testifies. Included
in this mountain is a vast quantity of critical prose, formal and informal,
published and unpublished, which is coextensive with his poetry in
subject-matter, function, and vigour.

For many years Pound's criticism was regarded as ephemeral, so that
T S Eliot in his 1954 Introduction to *Literary essays of Ezra Pound*
felt the need to justify the work historically and technically, pushing
that justification to a questionable point: 'What does seem to me true,
and necessary to say, is that Pound's critical writings, scattered and
occasional as they have been, form the *least dispensible* body of critical
writing in our time.' The sentence gives an impression of thinness which
is misleading. On the other hand, Eliot saw a truth which was then by
no means fully recognised: '. . . of no other poet can it be more important to say, that his criticism and his poetry, his precept and his practice,
compose a single *oeuvre*'. (LE, xiii) Since 1954, it has become normal
to turn to Pound's prose for assistance in interpreting the poetry,
since he often wrote about the same subject in both forms, and the

prose can help in identifying allusions. In introducing his edition of further prose material, William Cookson mentions 'the unity of Ezra Pound's vision and the integrity of his concerns' and describes the prose as 'statements of the beliefs from which he has made his poetry' (SPr, 7) without examining the assertion in any depth. Now, what this implies is that the poetry expresses a meaning which has been differently expressed in the prose; both have the same thing to say, in different forms, about the real world in which Pound lived and his experience of it. Both reflect Pound's vision and guide the reader to an interpretation of the poetry by means of the fullest comprehension of that reflection.

If we accept these assumptions, then Pound's prose essay is just one generic form of expression of his beliefs and emotions as a Canto is another form. Both provide an insight into Pound's intentional blueprint. From the standpoint of so expressive and realistic a set of criteria, there is no important distinction between the criticism and the poetry. On the other hand, it is clear that Pound himself valued his prose criticism much less than his poetry (LE, x); and an examination of typescripts shows him composing with a speed, carelessness and repetitiveness very different from his care in writing most of the poetry: he seems to have been willing to allow editors to revise the prose, whereas he retained control over the verse even to dictating its precise typographical layout. Second, Pound categorises his criticism according to method rather than subject matter, and this in itself suggests an attitude slightly inconsistent with the assumptions of expressive realism. Third, his ideas about the function of criticism move toward a theory of reading: a theory of readerly activity, which has both linguistic and social implications.

Pound found it both difficult and uncongenial to write long prose works. As he was completing *The spirit of romance*, he described in a letter[2] his sense that his own mental processes worked by sudden insights, or epigrammatic 'crystallisations', which he considered unsuited to the writing of consecutively structured prose. The letter reveals that he was planning future works of criticism in terms of very short pieces to introduce authors or his translations of their work; the 'Osiris' essays are close to the intentions outlined here (although in practice certain sections of 'Osiris' became more theoretically extended than Pound foresaw.) In fact, he published over five hundred essays and reviews during the London years, but of books, only *Gaudier-Brzeska* (1916), and sections of that were reprinted materials. Yet his published prose grew so extensive that when in about 1930 he thought of putting together an edition of 'Collected prose', Pound planned the project to run to no fewer than twelve volumes. In his general preface, he described his critical work in terms of language distinguished by its lack of rhyme and its undeveloped rhythmical patterns, and categorised it as either experimental prose (noting however that he was more interested in writing poetry), or work of publicising valuable authors, or indicative evidence of his having researched into the plenum of the literary tradition.[3] The most interesting thing about the preface is its evasiveness, and its description of criticism in linguistic terms, a kind of minimalist strategy for subjective documentation.

The essay, 'Date line', published in 1934 after the 'Collected prose' had been abandoned but perhaps the product of the work he had done on it, is Pound's most considered discussion of the theory and functions of literary criticism. It contains a confident and meaningful categorisation of criticism by method rather than either content or function; Pound distinguished:

'1 Criticism by discussion, extending from mere yatter, logic-chopping, and description of tendencies up to the clearly defined record of procedures and an attempt to formulate more or less general principles. . . .
2 Criticism by translation.
3 Criticism by exercise in the style of a given period. . . .
4 Criticism via music, meaning definitely the setting of a poet's words. . . . This is the most intense form of criticism save:
5 Criticism in new composition.'   (LE, 74-5)

The first describes most normal critical practice—reviewing, textual or formal analysis, historical and prescriptive criticism. Pound's casual formulation suggests his rather careless approach in fact; he was inclined to feel that finished annotation and comment might actually prevent a reader from achieving his own experience of a text.[4] The remaining four categories are more interesting. They refer to practices which are normally considered creative rather than critical; one is non-verbal; and the fifth in following from Pound's view of literary tradition and his efforts to 'Make it new', destroys the distinction between criticism and poetry in a way which echoes the 'Collected prose' preface very clearly. Here there is no *formal* distinction between the critical and the creative; and strategically the creative could be seen as *most* critical, in that he had recently defined the finest criticism as:

'. . . that which expresses the most profound and complete understanding of a subject. . . . So far removed is that complete knowledge which enables a man to act, from that partial knowledge which enables him to talk, even in an interesting manner, about any matter.'[5]

In theory, the first of the categories is the least important; in method it includes everything from fleeting comments embedded in letters or conversation, to the most developed and consistent book. Pound's methodology included both the 'clearly defined record of procedures' found in something like the long, annotative 1918 Henry James essay,

34

and the material on literary tradition culminating in the 1934 textbook-anthology *ABC of reading*. His essays — those of any length — normally use several such methodologies.

The remaining four categories all depend theoretically on Pound's firm belief that it is better to *demonstrate* understanding of a text than to talk around it. In the case of translation, he had learned from Rossetti that 'a translation remains perhaps the most direct form of commentary'.[6] The Cavalcanti translations of 1910, and Arnaut Daniel of 1911-2, already contain fairly sophisticated attempts to mirror the verse forms and sounds of the original, and by the time of the 1917-18 'Homage to Sextus Propertius', translation had moved so far beyond prose paraphrase that classical scholars denied it any status as translation, and Pound defended it as a work intended to be informative about the thought and language of the Roman poet and to translate the connotative elements of the original for a twentieth-century readership. By a variety of translating methods, Pound tried to demonstrate melopoeic and logopoeic elements of an original discourse.[7]

The third category — of exercise in the 'style of the period' — is of relatively minor importance, since Pound probably regarded the style of the period as a kind of symptomatic average of writing, or minor variation of the normal (LE, 23-4); but it was probably also the expression of the society or culture, and therefore not to be ignored by the serious critic if (equally) to be avoided by the serious creative artist. Pound was writing some such exercises during his last years in London, and some are reprinted in *Pavannes and divisions* (1918); but this is not material for his great, usable tradition. Pound's 'Imaginary letters' of 1917-18[8] might be taken as paradigm for this category, in their attempt to embody certain social and cultural attitudes of the period in the tone of the work, tone being a stylistic quality notoriously difficult for a critic to describe, but open to imitation and parody. They are however ephemeral, as parodies often are, and today resemble precious, fading photographs.

The fourth category, criticism by means of musical setting, retains the aim of communicating the critically-perceived essence of meaning. Pound's musical setting was an annotative mode of criticism. Music is used to clarify the subtleties of sound arising from the verbal surface of verse. It does so by emphasising the most important denotative elements of the text by means of an interaction, tonal and rhythmic, between the notes of the setting and the words of the text (including their rhythms and cadences). 'The music is to that extent a comment on, or an elucidation of, the form of the words and possibly of their meaning, or if you like, of the emotive contents' (GK, 366); and Pound's own operas, *Villon* and *Cavalcanti*, he described as 'concentrating . . . the audience's perception on the author's main meaning and not distracting

35

it to something less relevant, or to some minor element of the whole'.[9] It is probably right to see musical setting, in these terms, as analogous to criticism by translation.

The fifth mode − criticism in original work − is both the most important to Pound and the most problematic to the reader. It resembles the second and third modes both in the view of literature which it implies, and in the belief that understanding is really only demonstrated in the creative control of the material. All three categories are defined in the context of a literature which is seen as a tradition, or organic system: a synchronic body of applied language whose landmarks possess specific technical perfections available for re-use. Pound's example is T S Eliot's 'Fragment of an Agon' − '. . . infinitely more alive, more vigorous than his essay on Seneca', because Eliot has adapted the Senecan technique of verse dialogue to express his own perceptions: *technical control*, which is much more critical than any description of methods.

All five categories are alike, in that they are the methods of a poet-critic seeking, in the past, the elements of a usable tradition. This is the search which is summarised in the book of which 'Date line' formed the introduction and explanation: *Make it new* (1934). Descriptive criticism is subordinated throughout to experimental practices. The *authority* of a dogmatic descriptive practice is denied; but the validity of the perceptions of a practising poet is at the same time asserted. From the first, critics of Pound have noted the unusually literary nature of his poetry in its motivations, themes and sources. In essays like 'Date line' and the unpublished preface to 'Collected prose', Pound clarified his beliefs that the criticism of re-creation is the ultimate form of comment, and that criticism and poetry belong to the same phenomenological and logical order.

The functions of criticism

Having established his critical methodology in the first half of 'Date line', Pound then continued by considering function. He presents two terms: criticism is 'constructive' when associated with the self-conscious and experimental practice of art; and 'excernmental' when it evaluates and preserves the materials of the literary tradition.

Of constructive criticism, Pound wrote:

'Theoretically it tries to forerun composition, to serve as gunsight, though there is, I believe, no recorded instance of the foresight having EVER been of the slightest use save to actual composers. I mean the man who formulates any forward reach of co-ordinating principle is the man who produces the demonstration.' (LE, 75)

This is the poet talking − mumbling to himself as he works, studio notes. Finish is irrelevant to function. Pound himself preferred a rapid notational form of textual analysis and authorial survey, though it is true that he drew some general principles from specific instances. Of course there is an inherent inconsistency between the constructive function which Pound described and the actual publication of such criticism, especially if we accept Pound's judgement that creative writing is accomplished before the accompanying criticism is perhaps formulated, or certainly before it reaches publication (LE, 75). Pound effectively asserted that constructive criticism is superseded even as it appears, and that because it cannot be considered a final form, it is also rather limited in its expressive capacities — 'notes . . . usually in fairly unintelligible jargon, having a meaning for themselves [ie the authors] and for a very limited number of other people'.[10] It is the acceptance of mere unshaped 'yatter' as working notes which explains his low evaluation of descriptive or analytical criticism and throws a light on the kind of conventional, authoritarian, legislative criticism of essays like 'A few don'ts', published in the hope of helping younger writers to find short cuts in their own search for good craftsmanship (LE, 4-7). Constructive criticism is personal, informal and tactical, 'formulated as a method *to be used*' rather than 'dealt with narratively'.[11] Irresolvable inconsistencies, imprecision, notational incompleteness may be the normal faults of personal working notes because they are the close marginalia of the full statement, which is the aesthetic object. Yet when the notes are communicated, communication is necessarily incomplete. Pound appears to have devised a theory to explain the provisional quality of much of his own prose; yet the explanation does not justify our reading it. It may well be that the only fully constructive criticism is that contained within the poem itself, as in Pound's other four methodologies. For Pound, however, the incompleteness of technical notations is permitted because they are entirely ephemeral, and instantly corrected or completed in the poetic text which is the true end of the whole process, and which instantly outmodes them. For a reader to take such ephemera seriously, as law, abstract theory, or anything other than a progress report, is an error. 'Let it stand that the function of criticism is to efface itself when it has established it dissociations.' (LE, 80) To publish such work is illogical, although Pound seems to have thought of it as illuminating a historical process of writing (SR, 10) in which personal and progressive sense it can of course be seen as a record of the 'growth of the poet's mind' and skill, his purpose, meaning and practice.

The rules of so casual a mode are few. It is mainly positive rather than destructive because it seeks to distinguish the positive technical values which may be useful to others.[12] It avoids placing works on an evaluative scale, but rather seeks to distinguish different *kinds* of work.[13] Evaluation may be altogether abandoned, for Pound held that it is a duty of the constructive critic to recognise the positive values of a work which he personally dislikes, or of relatively minor authors.[14] In practice, his own literary criticism is usually positive: negative comments on technical matters are often brief and authoritarian, not so much a demonstration of something as a naked judgement stated firmly and passed by on the way to a different kind of positive value; and he accepts poor technique, or even objective errors, if he believes that an author's intentions are sincere and serious.[15] In one of his early discussions of the nature of criticism, Pound asserted that the critic should base his judgements on only four criteria: that the writer be 'serious', or culturally responsible; that he be achieving his intentions effectively; that his work be internally self-consistent; and that the style suit the message (PM, 46). His own criticism retained something of the openness that this highly problematic list requires. He tended to praise any poet who seemed to be taking himself seriously, and to recommend that his reader should go to the text. On the one hand, you 'forgive the poet his sins for the sake of his virtues', [16] and on the other, the serious artist must be seen to perceive and pursue the most productive of technical alternatives. The ends of reading are various, but the end of serious criticism is to encourage and develop the best possible new art, without reference to popular taste[17] — and for this the strategy which Pound pursued was positive.

What seems to follow from the idea of the 'constructive' is that critical practice remains impressionistic, and is validated objectively only by a demonstration of the writer's creative intelligence. Judgements are 'more or less proportionate to one's experience', and ultimately 'the critic can only say "I like it" or "I am moved"' (LE, 56). It is a curious conglomerate theory, at one and the same time deeply subjective and authoritarian in implications, and yet tentative in the sense of its validating tie with the creative work, the poem which is the end of the whole critical-creative process.

The second of the functional modes is what Pound called 'excernment':[18]

'The general ordering and weeding out of what has actually been performed. The elimination of repetitions. . . . The ordering of knowledge so that the next man (or generation) can most readily find the live part of it, and waste the least possible time among obsolete issues.' (LE, 75)

The biological connotations of the term, and Pound's emphasis on selection of significant detail, as by the gardener of his weeding image, suggest once more the organic and evolutionary nature of the tradition with which the critic works, and a developing theory of a *cultural* evolution: it is less *directly* associated with creative endeavour than the constructive mode, yet great poetry as Pound thought can only follow upon

38

the study of poetic media and traditions (SPr, 24), and because excernment takes a textual and technical approach to its work, it may
be addressed to the poet as well as the student. It publicises the unknown, places it within a tradition which its presence revises, and
revalues established works. Its methods are selective and comparative.
Pound's favourite analogy for excernment was the act of critical judgement exercised in hanging an exhibition of paintings in a museum. Its
function is didactic. Critical awareness develops through the process of
comparing the qualities of those paintings hung side by side, or of poems
similarly juxtaposed: the essential is to select, to make educated choices.[19]
In this way, editing an anthology is an act of criticism. Pound's various
anthologies of poems — *Des Imagistes* (1914), *Catholic anthology*
(1915), *Profile* (1932), *Active anthology* (1933) and *Confucius to
Cummings* (1964)[20] — should be considered as works of criticism, as
much as the *ABC of reading* (1934), where a commentary emphasises
the point by an exposition of method and its application to texts in
the English poetic tradition.[21]

Because the role of the excernmental critic is fundamentally selective and presentational, the quality of his judgement depends on the
adequacy of his previous knowledge, or critical education. The anthology
can also be seen as documentary evidence of this, since 'the worth of
the critic is known not by his arguments by by the quality of his choice'.
(SPr, 288) The preface to *Active anthology* is Pound's most sustained
defence of this principle. In agreeing here with T S Eliot's recently
reprinted views in 'Tradition and the individual talent', Pound suggested that the goal of criticism is to select from the organic tradition
'first the main form and main proportions of that order of extant letters,
to locate first the greater pyramids and then . . . the exact measure-
ments . . .'[22] That the ability to select well is at least as valuable as the
ability to express the basis of selection discursively, in formal prose, is
a permanent basis for Pound's critical approach. It goes back to the
method of 'luminous detail', announced in the 'Osiris' essays as a corrective to the useless generalisations of academic scholarship. From
The spirit of romance onward, Pound's heuristic method focused on
selecting historically-significant detail, or documents seen as representing and illuminating their literary-social cultural context, and therefore
more effective than the systems and categories of the descriptive critic,
who does everything for the reader, alienating the material from the
reader's personal experience.

To understand the peculiarities of Pound's own work as poet-critic, it
is necessary to understand what excernment implies. Even in 1910
Pound saw himself as seeking a new method of study which would take
all literature as of a piece (SR, 8). Dante's *De vulgari eloquentia* suggested
a model, for Dante's aim was to reform poetic method by examining

39

the work of a tradition, quoting significant texts and interspersing general comment with specific instances. Hence *The spirit of romance*, which makes some of the initial gestures of the academic period-survey (J W Mackail's *Latin literature*, a period-study in literary history for the general student, was a standard text during Pound's university years which he consulted while he was writing his own book[23]) shows the influence of Dante's critical methods in his mixing of technical concepts identified (however inadequately) by quotation of passages, with more general discussion, in a semi-analytical, semi-anthological approach. The chapter on Lope de Vega is excernment at its most mechanical — the naming of works by an under-rated author, with detail intended to direct the reader to the texts. With the exception of Camoens, the poets Pound writes about can be seen as 'generative' literary figures whose work he was soon to name 'donative' in literary tradition (SPr, 25). The hidden aim of the book is clear in excernmental terms: revelation of the nature of authorial *virtù*[43] by the presentation of selected interpretive examples of their 'donative' work.

The 'Osiris' essays extended Pound's methodology, including new landmarks like 'The seafarer', a translation presented without commentary as the first of the series to be published (CSP, 76-9). The series includes Pound's first metacritical discussion of the relation between the poem and the body of tradition, between the symptomatic text and that which supplies new resources to the whole. What Pound considered to be the 'donative' authors in the usable tradition came, from this point, to stand at the centre of his traditionalism; the prophetic brotherhood of artists mistily perceived in the earliest poetry is now being redefined in harder, more technical terms.

Because Pound held that no truly original or 'donative' text could entirely dissolve itself in the body of the tradition, a large part of his criticism began to consist of attempts to identify technical modes as they developed through the history of poetry. Of the essays adopting this particular focus, those which were reprinted in two collections, *Instigations* (1920) and *Make it new* (1934) — the names indicate the re-usable nature of tradition — remain the most interesting. Neither volume is casually structured, and *Make it new* is worth considering as an example of disciplined traditionalistic work, being a mature organisation of some of Pound's more formal kind of essay. After 'Date line' and its explanation of critical categories and methods, Pound organised 'Troubadours — their sorts and conditions' (1913) and 'Arnaut Daniel' (1920) with texts of eight poems, translations, and interstitial text dealing with technical devices. 'Notes on Elizabethan classicists' (1917-18) extends the usable tradition in time and space and examines the role of translation in traditionalism by a metacritical discussion, anthology of selections, annotation of some technical
40

procedures used in several languages, and heuristic theory dealing with the role of classical education in training the perception of humane values. As with its companion-piece, 'Translators of Greek' (1918-19), quotation and general discussion mingle. A study of modern French poetry adapted from the version in *The little review* (1918) (one of the few instances of Pound correcting prose) carries the book's theme forward in time, again with selections set into an annotative text. This is followed by a sub-section on prose — the essays on Henry James (1918) and Remy de Gourmont (1919). Unable to quote adequate and meaningful gobbets of prose text, Pound lists titles and comments on them briefly; he described this method as 'heterogeneous' (MIN, 316; also 325), and the essays do fail to give a reader any clear picture of the technical qualities of works which operate on the extended scale of narrative, so that an impression of superficiality is given which, especially in Gourmont's case, directly contradicts the argument of the essay. Both deal in general terms with the precision of prose social observation, and the section concludes logically, for this reason, with a historical document, 'A few don'ts by an Imagiste', from the period when Pound was urging that poets should adopt the *mot juste* of precise prose in order to reform the language of poetry. *Make it new* concludes achronologically with material from Pound's recently-published *Guido-Cavalcanti: rime* (1932), other Anglo-American publication arrangements having failed; the work examines poetic sound-patterns, and can presumably be seen as providing further material for young poets to study and understand in order to comprehend and make use of comparative values, in accordance with the title of the book.

The purpose of a collection like *Make it new* is much as with the more obviously didactic *ABC of reading*, published in the same year, with all its exercises and student tests. But *Make it new* is less explicitly didactic. It includes ALL methods of excernment: anthology, translation both excernmental and constructive in aim, allusion in booklists in 'Henry James' — all a making available of materials for workers in the tradition; and, finally, annotations requiring the reader to go to the original texts.

Pound's critical theory allows for a variety of excernment which mingles anthologising, translation and explication. To these should be added the simple booklists of the curricula for Iris Barry and other students, and the references and allusions of *Guide to Kulchur* (1938). There, Pound drew his material from both literary and social history in order to illustrate a tradition which is both aesthetic and ethical in terms suited to a very general readership. The product is one man's system of higher education, leading to the ability to evaluate the new in comparison with the achieved, to weigh Theocritus and Yeats in one scale (SR, 8). A simple list of names may become the equation for either an anthology

41

or an implicit formal criticism: 'Criticism may be written by a string of names: Confucius, Ovid and Homer, Villon, Corbière, Gautier.' (SPr, 288) Formal discourse vanishes; meaning belongs to allusion, to implication, to the gaps between words.

With the passing of time, Pound's writings increasingly denigrate the abstractions of an academic education. Excernmental presentation establishes a 'palette' of methods, of 'facts', and therefore 'we should develop a criticism of poetry based on world-poetry, on the work of maximum excellence.' (PM, 74-5; LE, 215, 225) By training the abstract faculty for criticism by close attention to one medium of art, excernment develops a general discrimination which can be applied to other arts. Therefore the end of excernment, like that of constructive criticism, is the extension of the tradition by new art comparable with the best of the old. But where constructive criticism deals directly with materials and techniques, excernment aims additionally at creating the cultural *conditions* — the learning, in general terms the map of culture or paideuma — necessary for new art. To discover the donative sources of poetic energy requires not merely a knowledge of the past, but clarification of a usable tradition which includes conceptual and emotional as well as technical sources of energy: the intensity which Pound associated with greatness. The product was the same, whether he was presenting it as the American Renaissance anticipated in *Patria mia* in 1912, the great Vortex of London in 1914, or the Paradiso which flickers in the *Cantos* and refuses ever entirely to go out. Excernment is not addressed only to the poet. Ultimately it aims at educating the public, at illuminating and emancipating the 'general intellectual life of the nation' (LE, 76).

Culture, tradition, translation

The organic relationship between the great donative poetry of the past and the creative complex of the twentieth-century Vortex suggests another of Pound's attitudes to tradition, or the culture. In this view, the body of tradition is analogous to the economic heritage of a nation perceived in terms of a fund of natural resources and social labour which may either be used to support a society, or wasted by neglect. Given this view of the literary heritage, it becomes easier to understand the objective basis for Pound's inclusion of creative modes among his critical methods. What he was saying about excernment most clearly makes this point. Pound sought a set of criteria whose validity was guaranteed by their objectivity. He mistrusted discursive criticism simply because of its relativity, that is, its notorious ability to give contradictory answers to the same problem. He was making this point when he misdescribed an anthology of poetry, *Profile* (1932), as a critical 'narrative', or outline of poetic achievement. *Active anthology*

(1933), its successor, was also presented as a means of informing readers of technical developments in twentieth-century verse.[24] This is to perceive criticism as though it were a series of details, like dots outlining a shape. The form or meaning of the whole is not contained in the individual point (which is dimensionless) but in the relationship between one dot and the others: that is, in the ellipse between the significant units. All Pound's anthologies of this period, from *ABC of reading* in which he makes an attempt to describe the relationships by means of narrative commentary, to *Active anthology* or *Make it new*, have a didactic aim embedded in the range of particulars presented: facts of linguistic usage, permanent values, in the work of the skilled craftsman and the presentation of it by the skilled critic (MIN, 7-8). Pound assumed that the problem was to force the reader, somehow, to abandon received opinions. To do so, he must avoid merely substituting his opinions for those of others. The experience of learning was, to Pound, always inductive, proceeding from closely-observed facts toward a synthesis.

Criticism becomes 'scientific' (always a term of praise in Pound's prose, associated with ideas of objectivity and precise observation of detail) insofar as it reproduces the particular objective phenomena for analysis and comparison. The critic's task is to discover these phenomena and present them; when they are unavailable because forgotten or misunderstood or merely extant in a language other than English, this can mean that he must act as editor, publicist, publisher, or translator. When he is dealing with a received literary canon he must re-examine and re-present such materials. In this task of de-familiarisation he also may become involved in methods which are not normally considered a part of literary criticism. Hence Pound's five methodological categories.

Given this theoretical and practical traditionalism, Pound's attitude to translation becomes interesting, as well as his methods. As his 'Notes on Elizabethan classicists' makes clear, Pound saw literary translation as a cultural activity important to periods of great original productivity (LE, 232). Translation can be regarded as a complex of methods of both presenting traditional material and demonstrating its modern significance, and is of value both to the culture and to the talented individual who is linked, by these means, to his artisitc tradition. Translation requires the translator to make a series of decisions about the ways in which both the formal or expressive qualities of the original text, and its connotative significance, can be communicated to readers who are historically and culturally very different from the original audience. Gaps in the understanding and interpretation of traditional texts are not merely a denotational gap; there are differences of context, linguistic codes, literary conventions, genres, social assumptions, and a whole cloud of associated meaning which hovers about language because of usages. Translation involves not just paraphrase, but the adjustment of linguistic codes. It is both the temporal and contextual adjustment of an old text, and may well involve the adjustment of poetic forms, in the sense of rhetorical ornaments, line lengths, rhyme schemes, and rhythmic patterns. The translator's decisions, therefore, are decisions about the nature of an equivalence which he is making, including the question of whether he will produce a version entirely contemporaneous by redefining *all* its terms, including the things like customs, values, which are presupposed by the text, not stated in it, or whether the adjustment should introduce a few cultural equivalents and leave present certain signs of the strangeness and pastness of the past — as for example when Pound decided to translate a section of the *Odyssey* into an Anglo-Saxon verse form and use it as a statement about tradition and cultural beginnings, in Canto 1. Any act of translation must naturally be selective, because it involves decisions as to which elements need to be re-communicated to a new audience, and how; as well as which need not, or cannot, be. This involves decisions as to whether the translation is to be treated as a new poem expressing the translator's experience of the original text, or merely as a key to unlock the old poem, perhaps even moving the reader to go to the original with a new ability to understand it, as Pound claimed for his *Homage to Sextus Propertius*.[25] Literal translation, or word-by-word paraphrase, can be thought of as a limited rendering of something which is sometimes called the 'prose sense' of a poem, its conceptual outline. This may be the first step in excernmental criticism, and some of Pound's early translation, as in *The spirit of romance*, was of this type. Here Pound was giving some version of texts which he had selected as historically and aesthetically valid, providing something at least for the monoglot reader. There is, perhaps, a carelessly expressionist basis for an assumption that the bare prose can in some way indicate the beauty of the original isolated from the unique form of its presentation.

However, by 1911 Pound was producing more liberal translations which partly mirror the literary expression of the original. Such formal equivalence can be seen as resembling technical analyses, or as the product of technical perceptions on the translator's part. With 'The seafarer' for example, which is one of those luminous details of the donative in literary tradition, Pound tries to mirror the cadences of the original poem. He uses its typically Anglo-Saxon rhythms, with the heavy caesural pause in each line; alliteration and kennings also appear in the translation. Pound's notorious mistranslations tend to echo the sound of the original rather than its literal meaning. In the first line, for instance, the homophonic translation of *'wrecan'* as 'reckon' rather than 'utter', or in line 37 'Moaneth' for *'monath'*, or 'urges', renders the sound of the original. There are other kinds of deliberate 'mistranslation' which remove Christianising references from the text and
44

return it to a pagan experience, which of course is a critical judgement of another kind.[26]

Such translation is what Pound called 'interpretive' (LE, 200) — work directed toward the original text with the aim of reflecting qualities of its content and expression in a way which makes them available to a new readership. A third kind — the imitation of 'impression' — is essentially a new poem. The relationship between the original and the impression is single in direction: the original text informs the imitation, but the imitation does not point toward the original so much as standing in independence of it. An example is found in the eight lines of Pound's 'Impressions of Fr Marie Arouet de Voltaire' (CSP, 185-6)[27] which are in a particular sense a translation of a thirty-six line poem; but they distil the original; and although Pound's lines stand in a logical relationship to the original, as the title indicates, it is problematic to argue that in any real sense they reproduce it. Impression, or 'homage' as Pound also called it,[28] is therefore a third kind of translator's reference to the original text, and clearly also an act of criticism.

Thus the role of translation in criticism varies. The reason that Pound abandoned the literal prose version was his perception that this mode actually fails to express very much of the original meaning. In the 1910 preface to *Sonnets and ballate of Guido Cavalcanti*, Pound speculated that poetry of a very distant time or culture might require translation of 'accompaniment', one which would communicate not merely literal denotative meanings, but the linguistic and cultural assumptions of the audience with whom the original had communicated. His own translations were still technically inadequate to follow up this perception, although the linguistic archaisms of Sonnet VII probably reveal less Pound's unconscious dependence on the language of Rossetti and his other Victorian models (which by 1912 he was trying consciously to overcome) than some attempt to choose and refer to an equivalent in received English poetic language for the expressions of an old, foreign and obscure poetry. He wrote of the dangers of misrepresenting the 'proportionate feel' of a text (Translations, 17; LE, 200). Interpretive translation is based, therefore, on a critical interpretation of an obscure text, and certain assumptions about the poet's original intentions.

A second interpretive mode focuses upon the representation in translation of specific technical qualities. The Arnaut Daniel translations, on which Pound worked from 1911 until publication in 1920, preserve and 'translate' intricate sound patterns (LE, 16; 16-24). In 'Can cai la fueilla' Pound reflects the caesural pauses, line- and half-line lengths, and stress patterns. Occasionally, as in 'Autet e bas', there are passages in which the vowel sounds of the translation also echo the originals. Obviously, such translations are developed to mirror the aural patterns

45

of the original texts because of Pound's perception of their special interest.[29] This interpretive mode, like the former, has the status of technical criticism in that they provide explications of specific expressive elements of the originals. The idea of translation of accompaniment also suggests the attempt to evoke an affect in the modern reader by a function equivalent to the affective function of the original. To do so might well require an insight into the imagined purposes of the original poet. In *Gaudier-Brzeska* (1916), writing of his *Personae* as a search for sincerity through the mask poems, Pound added that the process of the search continued in 'a long series of translations, which were but more elaborate masks' (GB, 98). In this light, the *persona* poems are a kind of translation of accompaniment: 'Sestina: Altaforte' just as much as the *Homage to Sextus Propertius.*

Propertius exemplifies a complex range of translation within a critical theory. Pound's Propertius 'is' Pound, the modern poet wearing the mask of the Roman's poetry, experiencing the other's experience, experiencing the other in his *phantastikon*. The perceptions of the two are juxtaposed in the poem. There is a translation of mental attitude in the ironies, which Pound had perceived in the Latin elegies, emphasised by selection, and reproduced in the linguistic codes of the 'homage'. Pound was asserting that the essential tone of the Propertian texts was the self-mocking awareness which we call irony. Secondly, he made a set of distinctions relating to Propertius's writing techniques. Translation of accompaniment communicates the relevant mental and emotional attitudes which he had decided were in the originals; it is the assertion that Propertius in the Roman Empire and Pound in the British agreed in their attitudes to certain values which the cultures possessed in common, and also in the literary forms suitable for the expression of their common views. Pound's translation was instantly attacked by classicists as literally faulty; he defended it by disclaiming any literal intention (Letters, 245-6), and the style of his *Homage*, which mirrors the Latin clause-order and therefore resembles the syntactically-disordered English phraseology of a schoolchild's translation, in fact simply flaunts the imprecision and linguistic clichés of conventional social attitudes to poetry and poets.

The *Homage* is a remaking of Propertius, like Pound's remaking of the odes of *The classic anthology defined by Confucius* (1954), or Sophocles's *Women of Trachis* (1956). All three are attempts to distinguish something of the quality of the diction of originals; their colloquialism in a classical literary context defamiliarises the work, defeats the reader's expectations, and renews the material in the twentieth century. Literal translation cannot accomplish these ends, and therefore does not achieve the status of critical comment. Interpretative translations of all kinds may fail by misleading the reader in respect of their

46

perceptions of original texts; they may put forward an interpretation which is eccentric, personal, and incapable of consistent support by reference to the original work. But so may all literary criticism. It is an error which literal translation, conducted on a level of paraphrasing competence, will not make. On the other hand, interpretative translation can succeed in translating, or communicating, the gestures of language of the original — connotative material expressed very incompletely, if at all, in the treatment of the linguistic material as though it were a simple denotative code.[30]

Pound's translations are both traditionalistic and critical in that they identify the capabilities of other texts and linguistic usages by means of his own, hovering on a half-defined boundary between translation and creation. If we accept Pound's view of literary criticism as experimental and practical, then *Propertius* must be seen as criticism in recreating the themes and linguistic usages of certain Latin poetry for English readers to whom the original is not available; or *Women of Trachis*, as a practical demonstration of the linguistic economy and intensity which Pound admired in Sophocles's Greek, as well as being a presentation of 'the highest peak of Greek sensibility registered' in Sophocles's drama.[31]

Translation can be seen as a critical task in the continuing cycle of the development and decadence of languages. Pound viewed the great classical Tudor translations as not only historical documents of English literature, but also the most recent, and therefore most meaningful, versions of certain verses available to the reader of his own time. So his own task in translating the work of, say, Cavalcanti was to renew linguistic codes which had been blurred by the usages of intervening centuries (Translations, 18). In preparing his edition of *Guido Cavalcanti: rime* between 1925 and 1938, Pound travelled to a number of Italian libraries, comparing manuscripts of the texts. His pocket notebooks show him moving from one version to another, clarifying his interpretations of specific words and phrases. The jottings suggest that his interest in commentaries was a practical concern for the meaning of obscure words and phrases, and there is no scholarly concern for an objectively preferred textual state; his working notes reveal ahistorical attitudes, and he was searching perhaps above all for the English *mot juste* apparently on the basis of his own critical preferences for the results.[32] His 'renewed' English versions are translation primarily in the sense that they communicate a pattern of *virtù* or energy seen by Pound in the originals.

A theory of traditionalistic translation hovers about affective criteria. Attention is focused on the imaginary modern reader with his own cultural habits of thought, and his own written dialect, requiring a translator-critic's equivalence for the experience undergone by the original reader. In translating *Women of Trachis*, Pound was conscious of

47

the example of Cocteau's *Antigone*, where modern diction and an emphasis on the contemporary nature of the content and motivation in the 'made-new' text give the 'SENSE of the play' as a dramatic entity, and place the twentieth-century audience in a position, vis-a-vis the translation, equivalent to that of the distant, ancient audience of the original performances. Translation overcomes a provincialism of attitudes to time and space, using the full resources of modern English and carrying out the changes necessary to create a corresponding quality in changed conditions (GK, 92-3).

The 'homage' is the culmination of the translator-critic's work. It is his detailed, pragmatic account of qualities of an original, the qualities distinguished by his educated critical judgement. The account is rendered more meaningful by being shifted from a possible descriptive analysis into an equivalent *creative* mode operating with the linguistic resources of the translator and his own culture. This equivalent embodies the translator's chosen emphases; it is the expression of his experience of the original linguistic object. It is likely to contain a balance of materials unlike that of the original for the same reason that I, in discussing Pound's work, emphasise some elements and ignore or devalue those which I perceive as less interesting or significant. The end of criticism is creative; the end of translation is perceptual renewal, re-use, furthering creation. Interpretative translation guides the reader into the *original*; the 'homage', as a translation of equivalence, turns the original into *something else* with the status of original work. Pound understood this well: 'Or is a fine poet ever translated until another his equal invents a new style in a later language.' (LE, 236) It is the range of possibilities as well as their nature which justifies Pound's placing it among the categories of criticism and which allies its purposes to the mode of excernment. Equally, it is the range which in some sense validates the excernmental aim of 'holding a torch for the public'. (LE, 349-50)

The limits of criticism

This image of the torch encapsulates the problem of Pound's methods and the theory beneath them. He holds a torch: he names luminous details and juxtaposes them in ways intended to imply, through their contiguity, a meaningful relationship. The juxtapositions actually mirror his personal experience of the detail. Yet as we have seen, the very idea of a re-usable artistic tradition implies a sophisticated model of tradition with a sufficient and necessary historical linking of its elements. To communicate the nature of such a system by presenting the exemplary elements whose connectiveness resides on the authority of the fact that *Ezra Pound had perceived and selected them* (in other words, an authoritative suggestion that meaningful links exist because a list or anthology has been produced) and that the meaning merely
48

awaits the efforts of the readers, for them to experience his experience of the thing, is to imply a highly phenomenological approach to the whole system.

Pound's literary criticism, insofar as it depends on such assumptions, forms one half of a critical dialogue between the master and the apprentice. The reader must supply certain responses, not merely to interpret the texts with which Pound presents him, but to supply the 'correct' unspoken relationships between the texts. What Pound demanded is for the readers to engage in an implicit Socratic dialogue with the critic; but because it is unspoken, not a real dialogue, the heuristic flexibility of the Socratic method is lacking. In this case the printed word is a somewhat rigid mode of exchange.

Take translation. Pound mentions 'transparent' translation: 'you can SEE the original through it'.[33] He wrote, of his work on Cavalcanti, that his strategy here was to drive the reader's understanding 'further into the original' than a more literal approach would do (LE, 172). This kind of statement about translation might pass unnoticed, so consistent is it with Pound's didactic assumptions. And yet the nature of the implied contract between translator, Pound, and reader here is a peculiar one in which 'mistranslation' (Pound called it 'atrocities': LE, 172) is justified by the translator's intentions. Translation is purposeful; it alludes to that purpose, but lacks the descriptive analysis which would meet the reader's expectations of argument and evidence, in the light of his normal expectations of common-sense denotative accuracy. Such analysis the reader himself must supply by surrendering to Pound's process and authority. In this, he must effectively accept that Pound's special purpose is based on an understanding more authoritative than his own, more completely educated. At the same time, by following this lead he may in the end join Pound in possession of that educated critical understanding, a mirror of the master's.

To go further: many of Pound's translations are critically motivated in that they contain self-conscious usages resembling identifiable forms and dictions within the body of English poetic tradition. They *allude* to the tradition by their techniques. Thus the archaisms of the translator's language may prove an *affective* equivalent; that is, an experience of the text by the new reader which is equivalent to that of the original by the readership intended by its author. When a translator like Pound writes in the idiom of the nineteenth century, or the ninth, for a twentieth-century audience, he is suggesting that the English material he echoes or alludes to is the closest cultural equivalent for that complex of linguistic codes by which the original communicated its meanings to the culture whose product it was.[34] He is translating signifiers. This is a critical as well as a creative practice. It has an effect of elucidating qualities by example, just as the critic would normally elucidate them

49

by descriptive analysis. But it does something which the purely textual analysis of formal criticism does not: it further implicates the literary tradition, that body of writing in which the original text and the modern translation are linked to one another. In other words, it makes a statement in the realms of literary history and literary sociology. The difficulty of course lies in the exemplary and allusive nature of the strategy, and also in the very subjective nature of the critical judgements which the translator has made from word to word. With a descriptive analysis, the reader sets criticism against text and gives or withholds his assent to the reading on a comparative basis. With a creative and allusive translation, there are so many logical ellipses that an evaluation of the critic's skill, and the granting of assent to his judgements and interpretations, becomes problematic.

Pound's version of the Confucian odes may be taken as an ultimate example of this difficulty. It is a useful one because of the availability of evidence of his working methods. As was his custom, Pound used a number of small notebooks[35] which record a series of decisions made in the selection of texts and slow development of English versions. The process begins with a rough translation of the four ideographs in each line of the original; the second and third attempts group these phrases syntactically to find more-colloquial equivalents for some peculiarly obscure and foreign images, and to experiment with rhyme schemes, moving toward an English form based roughly on the ballad stanza of English tradition.[36] In the end he achieves some cheerful equivalent, although in lines scrawled to himself in one of the notebooks, the ultimate incompleteness of translation is bluntly noted: 'real trans [lation] more to who knows orig[inal] than not'.[37] This follows from the nature of translation-as-criticism, because the reader who can compare the original and its renewal will discover for himself the nature of their equivalence, and the elements of the original which in the process are being distinguished. Even where the original and the translation are both available, however, as in Pound's edition of Cavalcanti, or any other parallel-text edition, the mode of discourse of a translation is radically different from that of descriptive analysis in the important respect that it entirely evades closure — closure in the sense of a single complete and unambiguous meaning. Where there are two authors, two texts and two audiences, and where the second of each is in self-conscious relationship with the first (a relationship qualified by the fact that the composition of the second was dominated by the existence of the first in the tradition), a multiplicity of meanings is created.

Pound's criticism constantly and repeatedly denied the validity of descriptive criticism. Instead, he asserted an overriding functionalism. It is the *effect* of criticism, not its message, which is important: that is, the behaviour which Pound saw the critical process as motivating in

50

terms of thought, investigation and new writing. Criticism and instruction are unified. The poet becomes a constructive critic through the simple fact of his need to develop his own writing within a literary and ahistorical tradition. The critic becomes a teacher in presenting his discoveries and criteria, by which presentation he controls the poetical education of his readers. Pound of course asserted that the 'mission' of the teacher is threefold: to maintain precise craftsmanship, to exercise his discrimination in the materials which he makes his subject-matter, and to discourage careless, abstract and received thought in those who read.[38] The first two roles are closely associated with the normal concerns of literary scholars and critics; the third was an aim as Pound insisted of good writing, prose or poetry linguistically clear and precise. The new method of literary criticism which Pound announced in 'Osiris' was of a selection and presentation of significant work from an international literary tradition, resulting in trans-cultural fertilisation; the search for and reproduction of this work is the purpose behind his surveys like 'How to read' (LE, 16) and perhaps all his important literary and cultural writings from 1929 onwards. And yet Pound also described this kind of work as the social service which an *artist* performs for his culture (LE, 58-9).

What is significant about this set of metacritical proposals is exactly the thing that Pound's critical practice reveals: there is a fusion of the functions of poet, critic and teacher. This fusion was implicit in his earliest essays, and remained probably the primary assumption of his prose work throughout over half a century, as well as one of the main effective motivations in the construction of the *Cantos*.

Literature and purpose
Pound's unification of the roles of critic, poet and teacher leads to the question of the aims of poetic discourse. In 1907 Pound told a friend that he was 'interested in art and extasy';[39] a decade later, he asserted that artists 'are the antennae of the race' (LE, 297). His development from ecstatic romantic expressionism to an awareness of a role for poetry in society was an aspect of that growing together of the poet's and the critic's functions. There are two aspects: at the psychological level, Pound considered that art affects the individual by presenting him with an intense, meaningful and illuminating experience; and at the social level art is both record and cleanser, and the very means of clarifying language itself.

At some time while he was at university, Pound came across a book by a mediaeval rhetorician, Rodolphus Agricola, which stated three aims of rhetoric: *'ut doceat, ut moveat, ut delectet'*.[40] Pound quoted the phrase in several essays; it became one of his pattern-imposing catch-phrases, and was applied to poetry rather than the formal rhetoric

51

which was its original object. His special interest in the tag lay in the authority that it gave his instinctive faith in emotion, ecstasy, in adding the role of *moving* the audience to the old, Aristotelian functions of teaching and pleasing. Logically, *ut moveat* is a middle term in the statement, and it is by no means clear that its function is not divided between the other two; but for the very young Ezra, with his personal acquiescence in Longinian transport associated with beauty and sublimity, the special emphasis was obviously important.

The preface to *The spirit of romance*, dated 1910, is a romantic statement of the value of art in life. Poetry is seen ahistorically, as an immortal, joyous thing whose effect intensely concerns the author (SR, 7-8). In the book, Pound repeatedly returned to questions of poetic intensity; only with Villon's subjective realism does the argument anticipate later concern with the truth of literature as a social record, a psychological record. Normally, at this time, Pound's statements of function emphasise the sublime:

'Great art is made to call forth, or create, an ecstasy. The finer the quality of this ecstasy, the finer the art. . . .' (SR, 82)

Greatness in art therefore produces ecstasy, Longinus's 'transport', a moment of psychological liberation and transcendence in the reader. If Pound later expressed such beliefs less urgently, he never really abandoned his faith in Longinian transport, *ut moveat*. It would be a mistake to think that he arrived at the modernism of his Imagism and Vorticism by abandoning the principle. Imagism involved a change of tactics, an emphasis on the formal techniques by which the old aims could be achieved; for Pound's image produces the 'sudden sense of liberation' which is Longinus's ecstatic transport, joined with the 'sense of growth', emotional or intellectual (LE, 4). Imagist statements about verbal clarity and precision should be seen against the older belief in moving by intensity.

The third classical function − *ut delectet*, to please − was of no concern to Pound; the interest of his functional ideas lies in the relationship between the other two elements. As early as the first of the 'Osiris' essays, Pound had begun to argue that the effects of poetry are not simply individual or personal, but social. Pound was attracted to Villon, whom he classified as a 'psychological' author − that is, one who is concerned to record human psychology. Pound argued in this connection that the aim of correct education is to develop the subject's understanding of his fellow humans, and that *this education is a function of serious art* (S Pr, 23; SR, 168-76). Poetry functions to alter the readers' perceptions, either offering meaningful alternatives to established habits of thought, or making them aware of the kind of originality associated with the peculiarly-creative imagination, the *virtù*, of
52

the great poet (S Pr, 24-31). It does not so much teach as identify and present the materials for learning.

Pound's conception of a poetry which communicates educationally but not didactically was developed in an essay published in 1913, 'The serious artist', which he described as his personal 'Defense of poesy' and which, like Sidney's, is a defense of literature from an ethical standpoint. The message of this essay is that serious literature is *the most sensitive record* of human experience:

'The arts, literature, poesy, are a science, just as chemistry is a science. Their subject is man. .... The arts give us a great percentage of the lasting and unassailable data regarding the nature of man . . . considered as a thinking and sentient creature.' (LE, 42)

This of course implies the scientific precision of the presentation of data; literature must be objective and representational in the sense of presenting both phenomenological and psychological data. Pound's terms bring together mimetic and expressive criteria, in a potential presentation of both external reality, and the poet's intellectual and emotional experience of it. The value of art is of course in its provision of what Pound considered the only objective basis for the development of social institutions. Bad art is redefined socially and ethically as 'false' art, immoral art. The essay voices a moralistic version of the old expressionist assumptions about the importance of the writer's intentions, his 'honesty' and 'sincerity'; and it associates these intentions with certain means of judgement: criteria like 'authenticity', and the touchstones, 'precision', 'passionate simplicity'. With its thoroughly moralistic bias, the essay develops a dualistic view of literature. On the one hand, Pound tells us, there is the 'art of cure' associated with the positive values of beauty; on the other, we have the negative, the delineation of ugliness which functions diagnostically. Both, Pound was arguing, must be objectively presented; for serious art is not didactic, it 'never asks anybody to do anything, or to think anything, or to be anything. It exists as the trees exist. . . . ' (LE, 46)

The purpose of literature, in the terms of Pound's current understanding, was to present the truth in such a way that the reader may trust the presentation and learn from it. It presents psychological data especially, as directly as possible; and the work is justified by the writer's ability to perceive reality clearly, and present it without distortion either intentional or accidental: both distortions are immoral. A direct consequence of this functional faith was Pound's theoretical focus, for the next decade, on the technical devices which allow this objectivity. Both Imagist and Vorticist work aimed at the representation of perceived truths and the defeat of received thought and inaccurate language, either which might blanket truth. The Image, presenting its

53

'intellectual and emotional complex in an instant of time', is psychologically swift, direct and undistorted: it communicates without subjective intervention. In Vorticism, the objectivity of the Image was extended to other arts, and for Pound at least the 'pure form' of Vorticist art was as much an educational weapon as an artistic tool. Again, the desire for objective truth lay behind the ideogrammic theory, which is a concept not merely of poetic technique but of educational methodology. All three major formal concepts of Pound's theory are in fact theories about the nature of the poetic event in terms of a moment of understanding in the reader's mind.[41]

Historically, Pound's emphasis on a social role for the teaching and moving function arose in his desire to promote an American cultural Renaissance. The 'Patria mia' essays which he published in *The new age* in the autumn of 1912 apply the aesthetic principles of the 'Osiris' series to the problem of an American art. A section of the series treats poetry as a mode of higher education, and the poet as champion of enlightened individualism, through the honesty of his human record (PM, 56-7 and *passim*). The essays develop Pound's idea of the poet's *virtù* and authority by giving him the social responsibility which is educational, economic and political. A few months afterwards, Pound was propagandising a Vorticist movement which was an artistic rebellion aimed at cultural change. The Vortex was the equivalent in society of the individual poet's *virtù*; BLAST attacked the lack of creative vitality in the previous generation of artists, and did so in the name of contemporaneity: 'To be civilized is to have a swift appreciation of the complicated life of today.'[42] Now the artist is seen as the receiving mechanism for social understanding (LE, 58). A few years later, when he became more interested in prose writers, Pound wrote of the author's labour for individual freedom: 'Artists are the antennae of the race ... the business of the artist is to make humanity more aware of itself.' (LE, 297)

Pound's development of a social concern can be seen in part as a result of his involvement with A R Orage's Guild Socialist weekly, *The new age*. Writers in Orage's circle introduced Pound to Confucian social ethics, with its concern for right government, and broadened his ideas about poetry's social functions.[43] By the end of the London years, in a series of *New age* articles entitled 'Provincialism the enemy', Pound was declaring his own war on ignorance and philistinism, and his aim of altering society and building the cultural Renaissance. In a sense, all his later writing, including both major critical prose like 'How to read' (1929) and *Guide to Kulchur* (1938), as well as his political and economic writings, and also the *Cantos* after their false start of 1915-17, must be seen in the light of this cultural purpose.

And yet Pound's growing and persistent concern with the educational and social functions of art did not mean that he abandoned the essentially individualistic direction of his earliest work. He saw the social world in terms of a collection of individuals, especially of leaders, and the educational functions of poetry in terms of the development of individualism, freedom of expression, and self-development. 'Civilisation is individual. The truth is individual'. (LE, 355) He did not perceive man as the product of his society except in the simplest way; rather, the individual is the single being standing in most respects *against* the evil collective pressures and oppressions of what Pound called 'provincialism' — ignorance, economic oppression, and the degenerate culture in which he must unhappily exist. The weight of Pound's early romanticism was of course elitist, as a poem like 'In durance' clearly reveals (CSP, 34-5). As the social emphasis strengthened, Pound began to make a trite distinction between the special individual who was an educable subject, and the ineducable masses: and then to slip gradually into accepting that the number of the educable might be both large and deserving, and finally by the mid-'thirties to address himself, in his various kinds of political writings, to a vaguely-conceived mass audience who were still receptive, though existing within the evil culture.[44]

Pound's concern for the social and educational functions was one of the things which led to his interest in prose, and especially the novel. Works like 'Patria mia' and especially 'The serious artist' reflect the influence of the man who was perhaps most responsible of all for the change: Ford Madox Hueffer, editor of *The English review* and one of Pound's first friends and mentors in London. It was Hueffer who made Pound take the novel seriously and who sent him to the French realists for models of a social approach. Hueffer's *The critical attitude*, published in 1911, is very much a product of the period when Pound was ripe for such influence. It outlines a set of attitudes which clearly underlie Pound's 'The serious artist', as well as most of what he had to say in later years about novels and novelists. It was Hueffer who argued that the novel provides objective psychological data, and that accurate presentation is essential to its function. Hueffer too uses the 'sincere' and the 'scientific' criteria to discuss the serious psychological realist, both terms central to Pound's similar arguments about poetry. For Hueffer, 'only in the mirror of the arts can any safety for the future of the state be found'.[45] Pound echoes:

'The permanent property . . . is precisely these data of the serious scientist and of the serious artist . . . as touching the nature of man, of individuals. No perfect state will be founded on the theory that all men are alike.' (LE, 47)

The emphasis in the individual, which had been seen in Pound's most youthful work, was supported by Hueffer and, a couple of years later, Wyndham Lewis; and so Pound developed his belief in the special critical intelligence of the artist, and in his attempt to 'drive' intelligence into the social mass.[46]

It was certainly Hueffer in the first instance who convinced Pound of the social validity of the novel. The idea of a 'scientific' social record derives ultimately from Hueffer's view of French realism and his interest in Flaubert. Between 1911 and 1920, Pound's interest in the novel, both French and Anglo-American, grew — always in the light of its 'diagnostic' social function. In 'The serious artist', Pound wrote about a method of social diagnosis, or of ugliness, and a method of therapy, of beauty, as in most poetry; but he did not entirely associate either 'method' solely with poetry or prose (LE, 20).[47] He considered both genres serious insofar as they record states of consciousness; but as 'Patria mia' had made clear, it is the novelist's function to direct his intelligence to rendering fact, whereas the 'steam-gauge' poet provides the measurement for human relationships, poetry being more dependent on emotion and — perhaps — less on logic (PM, 33). The 1918 essay on Henry James distinguishes more clearly between the novel, or prose generally, which is associated with a critical analysis of what is socially detestable, whereas poetry asserts the positive and beautiful. Poetry's values are emotional; prose analyses circumstance and is a mimetic rather than expressive mode (LE, 324n).

On balance, Pound's admonitions to poets tend to be technical, and to novelists, functional. A characteristic approach is to categorise poetry as language 'charged' with a variety of connotative energies; this is to view it as a mode of discourse,[48] which is why a moralist like F R Leavis could ignore the keenly moralistic element in Pound's work and attack it as obsessed with the technical.[49] It is almost as though Pound's strategy disconnects his views of the nature of poetry from his attitude to its function. Yet in 1936 Pound claimed that the basic criterion for *all* art is moral — though it was probably more typical when he announced to a correspondent in 1949 that 'all prose publication shd/be aimed at action'.[50]

It is in the light of his emphasis on the novel's *functions*, and Hueffer's influence on this, that we should see the arrival in Pound's essays of a concern for prose 'hardness' and the placing of French novelists as well as poets in his selected tradition of great literature. He began to measure English novelists against the French, the Flaubertian *mot juste*, and Realism's social recording. The long 1918 essay on Henry James, for example, pretends to be a survey but actually forms an emphatic argument for the novel as social diagnosis, although it says little of method (LE, 295-338).[51] Equally, Pound wrote of Wyndham Lewis as a social critic, and the long review of *Tarr* (LE, 424-30) shows little appreciation of the technical aspects of the work as opposed to its critical purpose. Even with James Joyce, whose work and artistry he constantly supported

56

and praised, what Pound most admired was its contribution to social enlightenment.[52] It is interesting that although his praise of Joyce's earlier social critique was unstinting (and largely unanalytical), Pound could see no good in *Finnegans wake*, although with its epic dream of history, its mythologising, its recurrent patterns of phrase and image, its allusiveness and polyglot nature, and its refusal of a closure of significance, this is the work which Pound's *Cantos* most resemble.

Despite Pound's theoretical respect for the work of certain novelists, he seems essentially to have been blind to prose structural elements like plot and character development, and his concentration on the diagnostic recording function in the novel's mimetic relationship to reality limited his understanding of prose, and his practice. At the end of the London years, Pound was writing a quantity of prose satire some of which was reprinted in the first section of *Pavannes and divisions* (1918). The 'Pavannes' includes parodies and satirical sketches written in admiration of the kind of 'active cerebration' which at that time he was praising in Wyndham Lewis, Rémy de Gourmont, and the W S Landor of *Imaginary conversations*. Pound's 'Imaginary letters' and other sketches of 1917-18 are a prose-fictional aspect of the impulse to social satire. Certain of the poems in *Lustra* (1916), like 'L'homme moyen sensuel' from *Pavannes and divisions* − an imitation of Byronic satire directed against current provincialisms − echo this impulse in verse forms. At the same period, Pound was writing a number of essays on writers, from Tudor translators to Henry James and Rémy de Gourmont, whom he regarded as having imported a breath of fresh air into the English provincialism which recurred from century to century. A number of these, with the addition of the 1913 essay, 'The serious artist', were reprinted in the 'Divisions' section of *Pavannes and divisions*, so that the book can be seen as a bi-partite statement of theory and example relating to Pound's current concerns with the forces of ignorance and cultural tyranny within contemporary society.

The 'Pavannes' satire was a cul-de-sac in Pound's development, although between 1916 and 1921 he persisted in writing original satirical prose. He was perhaps imitating Henry James, as he understood James. Pound's autobiographical 'Indiscretions' (1920), for example, was his professedly Jamesian attempt to 'render' the 'tone' of a culture,[53] and 'Imaginary letters', published in *The little review* during 1917 and 1918, at around the time of Pound's 'Henry James' issue, in part sought to present the causes of the war. This of course was also the period when Pound wrote his *Homage to Sextus Propertius* and *Hugh Selwyn Mauberley*. He described *Mauberley* as a verse-equivalent of a James novel (Letters, 248) partly intended for those who had misunderstood the aims of *Propertius*. Both these major poem sequences deal with the role of the poet in his society, and relate social degeneration and artistic failure. That was a theme which Pound also identified in Wyndham Lewis's novel, *Tarr*[54] and which also permeated the poetry of T S Eliot and the prose of James Joyce. Pound's major poetry of this period is probably best approached, therefore, against an understanding of his views on the social functions of art such as this, and of the cultural role of the serious artist.

Having determined that writing must function to assist social reform, Pound then distinguished two ways in which it might do so: the complex moral and psychological reform about which his ideas and emphasis changed from time to time, and the linguistic function. Pound understood thought to be a function of language (LE, 21-2). His attitudes were shaped by the principle which Dante had enunciated in *De vulgari eloquentia*: that poetry reforms language, that it develops the language and therefore the quality of thought iself within the culture.[55] In the London decade, when Pound associated linguistic reform and clarity of thought with social diagnosis, he linked this function with the precision of language in great poetry: the hard, the clear, the 'prose tradition of poetry' (LE, 424-30).

Any distinction which Pound could make between the socially-relevant mimetic content of the 'scientific' record, and the linguistically-relevant effects of valid *technique*, is blurred in his writings. While it is true that his emphasis on function increased during the 1930s,[56] his theory of literary tradition made a place for certain prose writings within the body of great art by ignoring literary structures in general and describing *all* literature in terms of language. His theory does not resemble a post-Saussurean structuralism, because it focuses on the sensual qualities of language rather than its signification. Words are 'charged' with non-conceptual significance, functioning to express states of consciousness (ABC, 36-40). Pound reduces all literature to language, and literary history becomes simply a record of a cycle of linguistic development in which diction develops a greater or lesser ability to fulfil its expressive function.[57] There is some evidence in Pound's work of an attempt to link good linguistic usage, ethical thought, and a good society, causally. One of his most persistent views, from the time of 'The wisdom of poetry' (1912) onward, is that language (which is the medium of thought) wears out as words draw away through over-use from the concrete things they signify, and becomes a conventional context, more or less entirely self-referential, or 'rhetorical'.[58] Pound's image of language was very simple; he thought of words as closely tied to the things which they signify — objects, actions. But they are like counters which wear smooth with use, communicating progressively smaller proportions of their original signification. However, 'rectification' (a term carrying both technical and moral overtones) or redefinition of terms could be achieved by the writer shifting

58

words into new contexts and relationships. This is an important theme of his later writing, and in the *Cantos* is represented not only by descriptive reference but by the catch-phrase, 'make it new' and the ideogram, *cheng-ming*. Linguistic renewal is associated with other forms of renewal: metamorphosis in poetry, the sudden complex of the Image, the energetic pattern of Vorticism — in all of which elements shift and re-form themselves into a renewed whole. This is associated with Confucian exhortations to social and linguistic renewal.

In Pound's Confucian translations, the structure of society is described as depending on its language, and to risk degenerative collapse 'if the terminology be not exact, if it fit not the thing. . . .'[59] But as early as the First World War, Pound had accepted that language is the basis for morality and that 'clear thought and sanity depend on clear prose. . . . The former produces the latter. The latter conserves and transmits the former.'[60] The popular linguistic practices of a country at war had probably encouraged Pound's proposal that 'if any human activity is sacred it is the formulation of thought in clear speech for the use of humanity. . . . '[61] The function of literature in society is a major theme of 'How to read':

'It has to do with the clarity and vigour of "any and every" thought and opinion. It has to do with maintaining the very cleanliness of the tools, the health of the very matter of thought itself.' (LE, 21)

This function is mechanical in the sense that it does not depend on a writer's personal morality but rather on his simple precision in using the linguistic tools of his craft. Here of course Pound's rather obscure interest in the 'style of the age' (LE, 23, 74) is justified in terms of a collective language which is impersonal, universal, perhaps precise, a conscious product of both traditional and contemporary usage, and peculiarly expressive of the whole culture. In Gourmont, Lewis and others, Pound admired a kind of *polumetis* mind aware of social complexities and capable of registering the complex tones of the period in their own expressive discourse.

Both Pound's criticism in the 1930s and onward, and the *Cantos* itself, are expressions of his tradition, compounded of literature, history and myth, and oriented toward an awareness of the ways in which language had been used at various times and in these contexts. His literary criticism, or 'excernment', can be seen as a historical examination of exemplary linguistic usage, and therefore an examination of the role of language in society (LE, 74-7), or of the relationship between literature, the connotations of words in contexts, and cultural vitality (PE, 4-5). Pound chose to redescribe the critical and literary achievements of the past. The poetic revolution of 1912-1920, the revolution which scholars have termed modernism, Pound described as 'scrutiny of the word, the cleaning up of syntax . . . in addition to, almost apart from, the question of content . . .' (S Pr, 291) Instead of the literary theories of a Hueffer, or an Eliot, Pound developed an interest in the Basic English of C K Ogden and I A Richards[61] as something tending to greater linguistic clarity and intensity. It is a concern which casts aside a dependence on richness, complexity and ambiguity of poetic language, and therefore the basic assumptions of the Anglo-American New Criticism.

To Pound, finally, literature was communication; and like freedom of transportation, or a flourishing economy, it was to liberate societies from inward-looking, provincial concerns. Literature is not just a representation of the society from which it arises and to which it addresses itself. Nor does it merely express that society in some more complex fashion. Rather, by linguistic usages, ways of blurring terms or clarifying them through redefinition, poetry reforms the very materials by which members of the society perceive the world around them; it works to 'rectify' intellectual and moral sensibility and thus to reform the basis of the culture. Language is the material of Pound's *paideuma* — 'the active element in the era, reaching into the next epoch, but conditioning actively all the thought and action of its own time'.[62] In its final, linguistic, function poetry has the double purpose of education and conservation: it educates individual perceptions through its affect on intellect and emotions (for Pound was essentially optimistic), thus affecting social relations; and, within society, it both records and analyses psychological data and by its experiments in linguistic expression which function to renew the meaningfulness of words, it reforms and vitalises ethic and thought. It preserves the best, makes it new, and applies it to the establishment of a new cultural order.

III

TEXT AND FORM

The energies of language

IN AN expressive theory of poetry, the 'truth' of poetic statement lies in the completeness with which it can be seen to coincide with and objectify the author's experience. A poet who is technically skilful will shape the work in a way which allows it to communicate that object-ified experience so *fully* that it becomes the reader's own, subjective fact. For every impulse there exists a potential for perfect expression, and for every reality, a completely suitable image in the appropriate form.

Pound began by assuming that poetry expresses the poet's thought and emotion, and that the vigour of that expression is the product of his *virtù*, or shaping energy. From this arise the questions how the poet can develop his skill so that the expression is perfect, and how a critic can recognise and evaluate such an accomplishment with any certainty. If we think of a poem as mirroring the world around us, then we can compare its reflection with the reality by using a concept of 'authenticity', meaning the clarity of the mirror-glass, its freedom from distortion. We will assume that common sense enables us to undertake the comparison, that likeness is a basis for both interpretation and evaluation; we might even wish to agree with the extreme mimetic suggestion that the 'greatest' art is the most lifelike illusion – the painted bowl of fruit which attracts the real wasp. On a scale of judge-ment, art is 'successful' insofar as it gives an illusion of unmediated reality.

But if, instead, we decide that it is the poet's purpose to reflect his subjective experience in the poem, rather than the objective world, then we are forced to question his *intention* in relation to the poem's meaning, and we go round and round in a circle – deducing intention from text, and evaluating text by coincidence with the presumed intention. Alternatively we may invoke affective criteria, say that a poem is great if it sends shivers up and down a spine – my spine, your spine – and lose ourselves in relativistic and subjective critical fisticuffs. We can also point to any formal elements which in themselves are capable of some kind of description and approach the question of

61

success in poetry by means of agreed standards of technique: this is a *good* poem because it is written in rhymed couplets (or free verse); or we propose moral standards in which the dominant culture is able to agree, and which oft was thought but ne'er so well expressed (with usura hath no man a house of good stone; what thou lovest well remains).

Pound's eclectic critical practice moved among all these possibilities at one time or another. His critical theory dealt largely with technical matters, and his attention to a usable tradition was voiced, as we have seen, in terms of discovery and formal development. Yet his many reviews, and the essays which he wrote on authors, very rarely proceed to analyse literary techniques, although they tend to contain dogmatic assertions about their use and usefulness.

We have also noted that Pound's earliest statements about art are idealistic, dealing with genius, the primacy of Beauty, and even the nature of Poetry as a quality independent of its physical form. Given all this, one of Pound's first evaluative measures was 'sincerity'. He used the term in *The spirit of romance*, for example, in referring to the integrity of the poet — his faithfulness to his mysterious personal vision, his unwavering determination to write in terms consistent with that vision (SR, 116). Villon was praised for 'unimaginative' sincerity in self-revelation (SR, 171). Sincere verse may of course be entirely in-stinctive: morally good without necessarily being skilful (LE, 44). Sincerity, for Pound as for many nineteenth century literary moralists, can be taken as a test of literary value; but Pound tended to treat sincerity in such a way as to make it seem verifiable by linking it with some requirement of special verbal precision. Thus for example one of the recurring symbols in the *Cantos* is the Confucian ideograph which Pound translated as ' "Sincerity". The precise definition of the word. . . .'[1] By this route, precision became for Pound the only guaran-tee of good art. To say this is, of course, merely to move the circular argument about sincerity into the more apparently-verifiable domain of language.

'Precision', as a word claiming to have meaning as a technical term, itself raised the same evaluative difficulties. Pound associated it with simplicity and directness of diction and syntax. Much of Pound's early poetic development, and much of his prescriptive criticism, concerns the reformation of poetic diction. As early as 1908, he foresaw his own poetic development toward simplicity and clarity (Letters, 39), and in the essay 'Prolegomena', written late in 1911, he described a new kind of poetry — hard, sane, true, austere and direct (LE, 11-12). There are signs of his rejection of the flowery diction of late-romantic verse, which he had come to see as expressing only received emotions, hence sentimentality, in the pages of *Ripostes* (1912), though his practice

62

was less consistent than his theory. Of course 1912 was the year of Imagisme, whose principles are those of direct treatment, conciseness, and the 'musical phrase' — all matters of poetic control, directness and brevity (LE, 3). From Ford Madox Hueffer, above all, Pound was learning the desirability of a 'prose tradition' in verse, or efficiency of writing (LE, 377) which sought to clear poetic discourse of received phraseology, so that a poem could articulate its own meaning in a controllable way, uncontaminated by either the subjective interpretations of the reader or any other external falsehoods.[2] In 'The serious artist':

'Roughly then, Good writing is writing that is perfectly controlled, the writer says just what he means. He says it with complete clarity and simplicity. He uses the smallest possible number of words.' (LE, 50)

Whether, as Pound here asserts, the poem expresses an emotional and subjective truth, or the novel an objective and social truth, only its precise formulation can justify the text (LE, 50, 71). The criterion of expressive precision assumes a moralistic imperative:

'The question of the fundamental accuracy of statement is the ONE sole morality of writing, as distinct from the morality of ideas discussed *in* the writing.'[3]

The spirit of traditionalism was for Pound in a search for a permanent reality, unmarred by imprecise and dishonest thought, feeling, expression. And the nature of truth in art is the subject-matter of many of Pound's poems, from 'Near Perigord' to the *Cantos*: the quest of art for a permanent truth in the flux of history. Perfect control and perfect accuracy hold truth, 'not mere succession of strokes, sightless narration' (*Cantos*, 7/24), to achieve 'that greatest quality of art, to wit, certitude'.[4]

This was Pound's way of answering the old Platonic objection that poetic truth and objective truth belong to different orders of reality. He assumed that the relation between sincerity and verbal precision is objectively (and therefore *experimentally*) verifiable. His adoption of a kind of pseudo-scientific vocabulary makes an implicit as well as explicit claim to this truth-status. As early as January 1912, in the 'Osiris' essays, Pound claimed that the proof of poetic truthfulness is objective, that the linguistic test is the only gauge of sincerity — a test which reckons the closeness of the word and the object which it signifies. Here he called the word a 'counter', a unitary physical reality precisely signifying a different physical reality: an explicit, verifiable self-consistency which underwrites the 'presentation method' of the 'prose tradition in verse'[5] — factual truth derived from the meaningful juxtaposition of these counter-words. The idea owes much to Ford Madox Hueffer's principle: 'Objectivity and again objectivity . . .'[6] When Pound, agreeing with Wyndham Lewis, wrote that art should '*have no* inside, nothing you cannot see. It is not something impelled . . . by a little ego-istic inside' (LE, 430) he was trying to abandon a clumsy romantic egoism by suggesting some alternative kind of art which consists in the *significant* accumulation of precise verbal codes, referring to concrete particulars with which the author's perceptions are wholly objectified. At this point his theory steps firmly past Romantic expressionism by emphasising the linguistic surface rather than the wellsprings of poetry.

Rejection of Romantic poetry and Romantic diction is enshrined in the poems of *Ripostes* (1912) and *Lustra* (1916). In the essays of the period Pound associated this rejection with a diversity of influences, including the clarity and objectivity of the verse of a number of French poets like Gautier, Corbière and Laforgue, Latin satire, and the poetic translations which he found in the notebooks of Ernest Fenellosa, the Japanese scholar, some of which he received during 1913. In addition, there were the exhortations of Hueffer — Pound claimed that in 1911 he rolled on the floor with laughter at the romantic rhetoric of Pound's *Canzoni*, but apparently he stood up and told Pound to learn clarity of the French novel.[7] There was also the slightly later example of T S Eliot's hard, dry work.

The Imagist movement which Pound established in 1912 should be seen primarily in terms of this strategy of reforming and modernising poetic discourse. The three principles on which Pound, H D and Richard Aldington were said to agree in that year were:

'1 Direct treatment of the 'thing' whether subjective or objective.
'2 To use absolutely no word that does not contribute to the presentation.
'3 As regarding rhythm: to compose in the sequence of the musical phrase, not in sequence of a metronome.'   (LE, 3)

The first two principles make certain assumptions: that reality, whether physical reality or the reality of the subjective experience, exists and is then 'treated' in language, and that a criterion (perhaps the most important criterion) of this treatment is a conjunction of brevity, clarity, and relevance. The third principle is correctly to be viewed as an afterthought, in the sense that it specifies a peculiarly *poetic* method of contributing to the relevance of presentation, for the rhythmic qualities of the verse also contribute to the presentation in an efficient manner.[8] Pound's Imagism may be distinguished from the Imagism of other 'Imagists' precisely because of this emphasis on directness and efficiency of expression.[9] Essentially, Pound had come to believe that the direct presentation of *fact* without subjective comment or description would produce a poetry which is objectively true. It communicates the factual essence, the quiddity, of external reality in its constatation. The hierarchy which is implied in 'How to read', for example, is based
64

on a notion of the primacy of linguistic values, and ignores problems of form or genre within literary tradition. If poetry is to be seen as 'language charged or energised' (LE, 25) then traditionalist criticism can be seen as a search for 'works where language is efficiently used' (LE, 23) and that alone. This is also why Pound's view of the tradition and his prescriptive criticism are based on an idea that diction develops through a cycle of invention, over-use and re-birth by new contextualisation, and why he perceived his youthful development in terms of a struggle to reform and modernise his own poetic language, a struggle against adopting the language of a Rossetti.

That struggle was profound. It involved Pound in self-consciously abandoning the acceptance of the developed diction of other poets — the bookish speech of his early writings — for a perceived naturalness and modernity (LE, 362).[11] Before the end of the London years, Pound had adopted from Remy de Gourmont the idea that '*Le style, c'est de sentir, de voir, de penser et rien de plus*'(LE, 354). That is, words cling so firmly to the mode of perception, to the truth as experienced by the individual, that the unreflecting adoption of another's diction can only render false the very attempt to communicate meaning (LE, 217, 286-7). Perception expresses itself not by derivative but interpretative language, words uniquely defined in context; the derivative *langue*, the 'style of the period' or of the preceding period, can only communicate 'the reaction of things on the writer, not a creative act *by* the writer'.[12] Ultimately this is why Hugh Selwyn Mauberley wrote with his seismograph rather than the critical sieve of precise language (CSP, 217).

Pound's linguistic precision was both sensory and semantic. 'The medium of poetry is words, ie conventional human symbols . . . capable of including things of nature, that is, sound quality, timbre, up to a point.'[13] In the years between writing *The spirit of romance* and discovering a language for the *Cantos*, Pound gradually developed a theory of linguistic categories in terms of the ways which he understood poetic language to be charged with meaning by sensory and conceptual means. His theory categorises language according to the source of this charge or energy. The system is laid out most fully in 'How to read' (1929), although Pound had approached it in a series of earlier essays:

'If we chuck out the classifications which apply to the outer shape of the work, or to its occasion, and if we look at what actually happens, in, let us say poetry, we will find that the language is charged or energised in various manners.

'That is to say, there are three "kinds of poetry": MELOPOEIA, wherein the words are charged, over and above their plain meaning, with some musical property, which directs the bearing or trend of that meaning.

'PHANOPOEIA, which is a casting of images upon the visual imagination.

'LOGOPOEIA, "the dance of the intellect among words", that is to say, it employs words not only for their direct meaning, but it takes count in a special way of habits of usage, of the context we *expect* to find with the word, its usual concomitants, of its known acceptances, and of ironical play. It holds the aesthetic content which is peculiarly the domain of verbal manifestation, and cannot possibly be contained in plastic or in music. It is the latest come, and perhaps most tricky and undependable mode.' (LE, 25)

There is, obviously, a logical gap between the statement that language is 'charged' in various ways with an extra-conceptual significance, and the statement that three types of poetry can be deduced in accordance with the modes of energising; many critics have objected to the limitations of the classification. F R Leavis, for example, was angered into making a published objection to the claim that such qualities of language are in practice distinguishable; he effectively rejected Pound's claim to alter the basis of critical investigation by treating linguistic classification as though it were an adequate approach to literature.[14] In conventional terms, Pound ignored both major form (which here he called the 'outer shape' of a work) and occasion, as well as the elements of subject-matter which interact with form and occasion to create the basis of literary genres — character, plot, theme, the elements which are the mimetic objects rather than the linguistic instrument. The approach also ignores the functionalist approach for the sake of close attention to linguistic usage. The classification which he was asserting so sweepingly here is more incomplete than he pretended; but what is interesting, from the viewpoint of the need to understand Pound's tactics as poet-critic, is his peculiarly linguistic approach to the art.

Poetry and sound: melopoeia

Pound's various statements to the effect that poetry is something more intense than prose can be related to an idea that it is the sound quality of verse which expresses the emotional basis of meaning. His first attitude to music was to think of it as wonderful, unconceptual, the vaguest of arts, and altogether concerned with emotion (Translations, 23). Of the critics who interested him as an undergraduate, Longinus considered music as a part of poetic expression and discussed its effect on an audience;[16] Dante dealt more technically with the sound patterns of verse. Both approaches formed part of Pound's earliest criticism.

In *The spirit of romance*, Pound identified pitch, or inarticulate sound, in poetry with the 'quality of voice' which is the vehicle of emotional import (SR, 160). This led him to a concept of what he

66

termed 'absolute rhythm', the manifestation of the poet's emotional energy. Absolute rhythm in poetry implies an entire form musically conceived which is unique in each different poem:

' . . . I believe in an ultimate and absolute rhythm as I believe in an absolute symbol or metaphor. The perception of the intellect is given in the word, that of the emotions in the cadence.
' . . . the rhythm of any poetic line corresponds to emotion. It is the poet's business that this correspondence be exact. . . .' (Translations, 23-4)

The term 'absolute rhythm' proposes a kind of metrical decorum, a propriety of relationship between emotional motivation and achieved rhythm. Metrical regularity is worthless, as is the regular stanza form associated with it, because a pre-determined aural quality cannot co-incide with the individual connotative message of the poem. In an expressive theory, it is reasonable to reject conventional metrical patterns on the grounds that they must warp the nature of the expression, so that emotional import is lost. By 1910 Pound had therefore already begun to argue that there are differences in *meaning* between verses governed by the 'surge and sway' of a smooth, Swinburnean cadence, and the distinctive arrangement of irregular accents and variable cadences in the less *cantabile* verse of Burns (SR, 161). Euphonious verses, with regular metres and a pleasant play of vowels, are normally considered melodious, but Pound was already beginning to speculate about a poetic music in which monosyllabic textures and heavy stress patterns form a more significant cumulative rhythm, as in Browning's poetry, which influenced his own techniques.[17] By 1912, therefore, Pound had decided that a poet must have his own rhythm and that it must be 'interpretative' and inimitable (LE, 9).

Pound himself experimented with a variety of conventional metres and stanza forms, as the old story of his self-imposed task of writing a sonnet a day for a year indicates. Even in 1908, however, *A Lume Spento* contained many experiments with irregular stress, as well as the many verses based on the dactylic and spondaic foot: Pound was breaking the iambic pentameter by following Browning's model, using sharp, abrupt accents and heavily stressed monosyllables. Edward Thomas, the English poet who wrote the most perceptive of the reviews of *Personae* in 1909, especially noted the interest of the metrical experiments in the volume. The 1911 *Canzoni* was overwhelmed by this kind of work. That collection is almost worthless except for the interest of the ways in which Pound was developing sound-patterns (he dropped the poems from later selections of his work). Next, the translations of Arnaut Daniel's verses, which are the centre of the 'Osiris' essays, repeated the metrical experiments. From the Arnaut texts as from

67

Dante's *De vulgari eloquentia*, Pound was learning that rhyme is a musical element and that a sequence of rhymed stanzas forms a pattern of echoes, a sound-pattern lasting for the duration of the text (SR, 38; LE, 6-7). This aural persistence was something which became very important to Pound's musical theory, and his later translations of Arnaut were still struggling with it. In translating 'Autet e bas entrals prims fuoills', for instance, Pound's retention of a pattern of -*us* endings in the fifth and sixth lines of each stanza forms an onomatapoeic '*cadahus*' bird-song (LE, 124-7). With 'L'aura amara', he was imitating line lengths, stresses, even to some extent the vowel sounds of the original text, and producing not a simple translation of denotation, but an English equivalent of sound and meaning:

L'aura amara	The bitter air
Fals bruoills brancutz	Strips panoply
Clarzir	From trees
Quel doutz espeissa ab fuoills,	Where softer winds set leaves,
Els letz	The glad
Becs	Beaks
Dels auzels ramencs	Now in breaks are coy
Ten balps e mutz	Scarce peeps the wee
Pars	Mates
E non pars . . .	An un-mates . . . (LE, 127-8)

Much of Pound's early melopoeic study was in Provençal poetry, verse in an uninflected language (like English) whose metrical formations could therefore be compared with English usages. Provençal verse seemed to provide a more 'usable' technical example than the inflected language and quantitative forms of the Greek verse in whose sound qualities he took intense pleasure.

Interest in the concept of absolute rhythm and in Pound's early metrical experiments should not obscure the fact that his melopoeic theory encompassed more than metre, and moved beyond simple emotional expression. Certainly his earliest thinking about verse music (SPr, 35-40) dealt with both rhythm and pitch. In the 'Osiris' essays he put forward the idea of a musical period in verse – a sound-unit extending beyond the single line to produce a naturally irregular line-length and a metre based on the poet's breath-length (hence the inimitable nature of the sound-unit) and natural vocal stress. Such a line possesses an inner form rather than an imposed shape. As examples Pound referred to Yeats and – interestingly, for it is his only word of approval – Milton as the great English-language masters of the musical period. Secondly, based on this idea of the natural line, there is a concept of tone-leading, or the arousal of an expectation in the reader's aural imagination of the shape and sound-patterns which are in the process of being developed.

68

Tone-leading arises extensively, of course, in the case of regular metres and stanza forms, for the ear expects an established rhythm to continue. But Pound has abandoned this easy expectation, and his version of tone-leading depends on a system of overtones, cadences: a music which consists not of regular beats or stressed feet, but of articulate sound in the sense of a sequence of vowels and consonants with rising and falling inflections (SPr, 39). Without working out the full implications of this approach, Pound was already approaching the Imagist idea of complex aural verse systems, the energy defined in relation to the purely conceptual aspect of the 'prose' word as *melopoeia*, 'wherein the words are charged . . . with some musical property, which directs the bearing or trend of that meaning'. (LE, 25)

Pound's work on the poetry of Guido Cavalcanti, begun for *The spirit of romance* and culminating two decades later in his edition of *Guido Cavalcanti: rime*, developed the concept of an absolute rhythm, directly involved in the original text and incapable of ordinary translation (LE, 167-73, 195-200). Versions of Sonnet VII ('Who is she that comes') and 'Donna mi prega' are his most serious attempts at a melopoeic equivalent which will render the *cantabile* quality of the original discourse, a quality largely produced by rhyming echoes (LE, 170). Pound perceived a coincidence of sound and meaning within each phrase-unit and broke up Cavalcanti's longer line to show something of the free, rhythmical phrasing within it (LE, 163-7, 168).

Imagism, in terms of the literary movement which Pound was 'inventing' and propagandising between 1912 and 1914, tends to be misunderstood because for a long time scholars emphasised the visual qualities of the poetic image.[18] Yet two of the three Imagist principles in 'A few don'ts', the Imagist manifesto, relate to verbal precision while the third and most specific is the principle of absolute rhythm, or inner form of the line: 'As regarding rhythm: to compose in the sequence of the musical phrase, not in sequence of a metronome.' (LE, 3)[19] This required the abandonment of mechanical repetitive devices in favour of natural spoken verse-units coinciding with conceptual units and probably also (Pound's theory is not entirely clear about this, although his reading practice strongly supports it) with breath-units. The apparent move toward free verse was actually part of a search for a mode of *quantitative* verse which, unlike Classical quantitative line forms, could be used for poetry in the English language.[20]

Much of Pound's work, in the two years of his Imagism, was propaganda for the third principle. His essay, 'The tradition', for instance is largely a defence of poets who have written 'to the feel of the thing, to the cadence' (LE, 92-3), and exemplars are drawn from literary periods when, as Pound believed, poetry and music were closely associated, as in the Troubadour verse of Provence. This is the basis for Pound's evaluation of the English poetic tradition, with his praise for the poetry of the centuries from Chaucer to Johnson in which, as he maintained, vowel sequences combined in clear musical cadences, and metre was made to coincide with natural stress; and damning 'Milton and Victorianism and . . . the softness of the 'nineties' (LE, 362) not for moralism or didacticism, but for their disjunction between the sound of the words in the verse context, and the natural sound of the diction. From his initial (and really quite correct) respect for the flexible Miltonic verse-paragraph, he had moved to condemn it because he saw in this verse the syntax appropriate to an inflected language, and an associated prosody which piles sound grandly on sound; and he believed that both tend to obscure the real meaning of the words (LE, 237-8). His rejection of Milton and the Miltonic was a rejection of all the sonorous poets who had influenced his own romantic verses, with the exception only of Yeats who (at least after 1910) had worked to achieve his own possession of a new music (LE, 378).

Cultivation of the musical phrase as the absolute rhythm of poetic significance was Pound's personal attempt to abandon the iambic foot, to cultivate a unique melopoeia.[21] *Ripostes* (1912), *Cathay* (1915) and *Lustra* (1916) document the effort. The more extensive experiments Pound made were directly related to his concept of 'inner form' and melopoeic connotation. At one end of his range is a poem like 'Dance figure' in *Lustra* which is Pound's own example of the heavily-stressed free verse (LE, 12):

> 'Dark eyed
> O woman of my dreams,
> Ivory sandaled,
> There is none like thee among the dancers,
> None with swift feet.'   (CSP, 99)

Physical movement is communicated by a mixture of stresses, the pauses induced by the close proximity of several heavy stresses, and line breaks, and the comparatively smooth elisions of lines two and four. There is no marked distinction between the vowels and consonants of the two smooth lines, and those of the heavily-stressed group. Neither the conceptual nor the visual elements of the stanza are remarkable: its interest is its rhythm, as Pound himself was aware: meaning resides largely in its imitation of the gestures of dancing which it describes. Other poems — 'Apparuit', 'The return', 'Effects of music upon a company of people' — which were chosen by Pound as representing 'more tenuous and imperceptible rhythms' — depend less heavily on stress:

> 'See, they return; ah, see the tentative
> Movements, and the slow feet,
> The trouble in the pace and the uncertain
> Wavering!'   (CSP, 85)

Here the succession of long and short vowel sounds, with the run-on first and third lines, creates an illusion of hesitant movement which is also the overt subject of the poem. This free verse is not an abandonment of an appropriate form, but the assumption of added precision in both melodic and referential elements. Signification here assumes both aural and conceptual qualities.

The usual criticism of Pound's melopoeic theory is that it attempts to separate sound from sense. It is true that from time to time he recommended that a young poet should fill his mind's ear with beautiful cadences, ignoring sense to concentrate on sound; and also that he has written of such aspects of the sound of poetry as assonance, alliteration and rhyme patterns *as though* writing of the techniques of musical composition rather than a conceptual medium (LE, 5, 6). But it is equally clear that this kind of advice is technical and programmatic — advice for the apprentice poet equivalent to the advice that a student of the piano should practise his scales. It is clear from both the theory itself and the poetic examples which Pound presented that he was concerned to enhance not merely the expressive, but the significative diction of the poem.

Another confusion arises from Pound's association of poetry — specifically the aural qualities of poetic language — with music. This confusion is very real. Pound himself was interested in music of a certain kind, and worked as impressario, music reviewer, and composer. His first guide to the writing of poetry (which as late as 1950 he described as 'still' the only useful guide to rhetoric[22]) was Dante's *De vulgari eloquentia*. Dante's treatise describes poetry as *'Fictio rethorica musica poita'*,[23] for he was concerned with poetry written to be sung, and I suspect that there is an unspoken extension of this very special concern colouring Pound's thinking. Assuming that poetry is intended to be read aloud, and heard, the arts of poetry and music do share certain physical properties of pitch and cadence. Pound's own interest in song was very real, whether they were the songs of his beloved troubadours, or the songs sung in the London concert-halls during the years 1917-1921 when, under the pseudonym of William Atheling, Pound regularly reviewed music for *The new age* and had a good deal to say about the need to set words to music in such a way as to clarify and augment the rhythms of the words, or to emphasise the significant portions of verse and amplify the verbal meaning.[24] Atheling's priorities were really a poet's priorities, for his reviews invariably give primacy to the words rather than the harmonic line, and he always deplored any distortion of verbal values by the musical setting. The singer's voice, too, he regarded as a means of communication rather than a musical instrument. Again, Pound divided melopoeia into three categories: poetry made to be spoken, to be chanted, to be sung (LE, 167); he composed

71

operas in which the musical setting conforms to his criteria for enhancing words; he was interested enough in the 'new music' of Yeats to record the sound of the poet's chanting in Canto 83 (a sound which he sometimes imitated in reading his own work[25]): but despite all this, the fact remains that his taste took him, in his search for a music which would not distort verbal values, to the monodic, linear, unharmonic forms of seventeenth century music, and to the approximations of poetic and musical rhythms of a composer like Henry Lawes.[26]

In the English language, syllabic stress depends in part on the natural pronunciation of the words (which is in turn largely related to vowel lenth) and in part on the way in which rhythm forms patterns of expectation in the listener. Pound understood stress and duration to be somewhat independent of one another, and variable, as well as being affected by the cadences imposed by a musical accompaniment.[27] In *De vulgari eloquentia*, Dante described the sounds of words as 'combed', 'shaggy' and 'oily': the distinctions mean little to the modern English-speaker but are in accord with the number of syllables in a line of verse, an the presence or absence of aspirates, double consonants, and liquid and mute sounds.[28] Pound's discussion of aural textures of English, and the melopoeia of sound duration and variable stress (LE, 114) are influenced by Dante's categories. He also adopted Dante's musical theory, dealing with the succession and weight of syllables, the sounds of words singly and combined within the line of verse, and the sound of the stanza as a unit, a repetitive sound-pattern based on quantity (the length of syllables and lines) and pattern (rhyme). In Dante's examples, the structural arrangement was of course limited by the musical pattern — the tune of the accompaniment.

What Pound attempted to do was apply Dante's conclusions of a specialised study of song, to poetry in general. He began to use Provençal poetry as a melopoeic touchstone, and a body of material full of techniques and examples. Of this tradition, Arnaut Daniel's poetry was the most full of patterned stanza arrangements, rhyme echoes, the untranslatable melopoeia of a specific word order, syllabic duration, and pitch which varies with syntax and stress. Such qualities do not remain constant throughout the centuries even within the English language, and they do not easily translate (LE, 25, 168-9). Nevertheless, his study of Daniel reinforced his concern with the reform of diction, the development of a precise melopoeia as a part of poetic signification, and the consequential movement of his poetic theory and strategy away from expressionist emphases, and towards the belief in the organic unity of the poem, and a formalist critique. It contributed to his perception of poetry as a linguistic text, a particular form of discourse whose elements of duration and order make a design *in time* (ABC, 202-3). That is, the design of a poem is seen as a sequential combination of interrelated

72

sounds. It is here that rhythm, as the emotionally-expressive quality, unites with cadence in an absolute linguistic reference which expresses conceptual meaning: Imagism's 'sound-unit' principle.[29]

As Pound's Vorticism developed from his Imagist theories, and he attempted to broaden his musical theory in his 'Treatise on harmony' (1921), he retained his definition of music as an interaction of rhythms and echoing overtones. Murray Schafer, who has made a study of Pound's music, describes[30] his developing theory of absolute rhythm and the 'great bass' as a method of organising detail, a device in which the mathematical regularities of metre, and the organic shapes of art, are related and mutually varied. It is this relation between the fixed element and the variable which is ultimately the most interesting and important aspect of Pound's theory, and a basis for understanding the aural qualities of the *Cantos*.

The effect of Pound's ideas about pitch[31] is to emphasise the interacting unity of sound in an entire composition. His conception of form in poetry is analogous to that in this view of musical composition. The idea of form as a complex of sound, a kind of extended internal echo (Pound called this the 'Great Bass', in music), is the product of his melopoeic theories. From the patterns echoing in Arnaut's poems, to the poetic 'cross run of the beat and the word' in the work of James Joyce, (LE, 413) poetry as sound 'caught in the unstopped ear' against a developing expectancy (CSP, 205) provides us with a way of approaching and understanding the compositional principle of his own writing, and above all of the old problem of the structure of the *Cantos*.

By 1920, Pound was entirely aware of the structural and expressive problems of the *Cantos* project he had undertaken. In a letter to the *Dial*, published in December 1920, he wrote of two means of indicating tone and rhythm in verse: musical accompaniment and typography.[32] It was not possible to use music very extensively in a poem of great length (although Canto 75 is a song, and Canto 91 contains a few notes), but he turned to Robert de Souza's *Terpsichore*, with its broken lines and italicised phrases, and to Henri-Martin Barzun's 'polyphonic' method, the 'orchestral' use of 'voices' with 'solos' of thought as models for a kind of writing analogous to his musical forms.[33] After about 1920, Pound's verse became more and more visually eccentric in the effort to score a verbal symphony. The arrangement of words on paper affects the speed of a reading and the position of the pauses. Typography, in word and line division and positioning, indicates effects too dependent on the aural to be adequately represented by conventional punctuation (Letters, 418). Corrected page proofs of Cantos show an attention by both Pound himself and editors to the precise indentation of lines. Blanks within or between lines and passages create pauses of varying length, breaking and replacing conventional syntax and punctuation.

73

Where standard English syntax is abandoned as a principle of verbal organisation (and this poetry is essentially asyntactical), the verse movement carries a proportion of its significance, especially that part of meaning which is implied in the relationship of one verbal unit to another. The communicated meaning of Canto 1 includes the special associations, for the Anglo-American reader, of its heavily-accented, caesural, Anglo-Saxon epic line: meaning here is in a cultural comparison signified by the line. Phonetic irregularities indicating dialect English operate in a similar way. So does the literary dialect with its extremely rhythmical support in Canto 45, the Usura canto, where the moral message is culturally defined by the heavily stressed, repetitive chant, with its variable foot and rising inflection; the sound, associated with the historically-specific vocabulary, relates the conceptual message to that of the Authorised Version of the Bible. Here, the melopoeia energizes the codified meaning of the words, so that the relationship between art and morality is strongly signified by the language of the poem.

There are many passages, perhaps most notably in the *Pisan cantos*, where cadences and rhythms build to a chant with ecstatic religious significance, expressing the mystical revelations of lost chthonic myth. The construction of recurring sounds (and images) of Canto 90 provides a useful example of this in a complex sound pattern beginning with the regular chant —

> '... Sibylla,
> from under the rubble heap
>   m'elevasti
> from the dulled edge beyond pain
>   m'elevasti
> out of Erberus the deep-lying
>   from the wind under the earth
>   m'elevasti ...

and breaking into the irregularities of the final section, beginning 'Grove hath its altar' and rising in the typically Poundian prosody of broken lines to the ultimate vision:

> 'For the procession of Corpus
>   come now banners
>   comes flute tone
>   *oi chthonioi*
>   to new forest
>   thick smoke, purple, rising
>   bright flame now on the altar
>   the crystal funnel of air
>   out of Erberus, the delivered,

```
                    Tyro, Alcmene, free now, ascending
e i cavalieri,
                    ascending,
no shades more,
            lights among them, enkindled,
and the dark shade of courage
                    Electra
bowed still with the wrongs of Aegisthus.
Trees die & the dream remains
                    Not live but that love flows from it
                    ex animo
                    & cannot ergo delight in itself
                    but only in the love flowing from it.
      UBI AMOR IBI OCULUS EST.'      (Cantos, 90/606-8)
```

The whole passage, with its stresses, repetition and rhythmically-defined units, the coincidence of breath-phrases with images, and the significant lengthening of pauses between units, is a complex of melopoeia. The poem does not merely *say*, it *is*: and to receive its full significance one must at least hear it in the mind's ear.

Form and image
During the decade from about 1910 to 1920, then, Pound's prescriptive and traditionalistic criticism was directed toward identifying and achieving linguistic precision and hence the intensity which he held to be essential to good poetry. The movements — Imagism and Vorticism — as well as much of Pound's more personal practice, are all aspects of this reformation of poetry and poetic language. Pound began by believing that the music of verse was the expression of emotional intensity, but as he drifted away from his early expressionist attitudes, he began to think of melopoeia as an energy which could lead toward a pre-conceptual, unliterary, 'unthinking sentient' expressed in the non-verbal 'primary pigment' of pure music.[34] The change was logically inconsistent with his continuing assertions about absolute rhythm and *its* precision, and that inconsistency cannot be resolved. However it may have been both this ambivalent attitude to music, and his perception that melopoeia did not wholly account for the energies of the poetic text, that led Pound to clarify his understanding of the language of poetry. Beside melopoeia he placed 'phanopoeia' — a casting of images upon the visual imagination', and by the time that he was laying out his categories in 'How to read' (1929), he had decided that in phanopoeia there lay the strongest impulse to verbal precision (LE, 25-6).

In *The spirit of romance*, there are several interesting discussions of the visual imagery of Dante and Shakespeare (SR, 126-63). That imagery

75

consists of both concrete epithets ('Primary apparitions') and metaphors — the elliptical presentations of experience with visual elements (SR, 158-9). However, there is a remarkable poverty of visual imagery in his own verse of the period. Although his earliest poems are often descriptive in their strategy, they are actually vague except for certain notable colour imagery. Where his work superficially resembles Pre-Raphaelite pictorialism, even here it is obviously less concrete. This can easily be judged by comparing Pound's poem, 'Donzella beata', with the work which it answers, Rossetti's 'Blessed damosel'. Rossetti's lady, leaning in a notoriously fleshly manner on the bar of heaven, is as concretely presented as an oil portrait. Pound's donzella is not pictured, but *addressed* by her lover in the most abstract of vocatives:

> 'Soul
> Caught in the rose-hued mesh
> Of o'er fair earthly flesh,
> Stooped you this thing to bear
> Again for me? And be
> Rare light to me, gold-white
> In the shadowy path I tread?   (ALS, 41)

The work is unfocused. The apparently-specific 'rose-hued' turns out to be metaphorically applied to the 'mesh' rather than the concrete of 'flesh'; 'this thing' (flesh? life? sin?) refuses definition; and the path, being 'shadowy', is safely indescribable.

However, in considering Shakespeare and Dante, Pound was well aware of the precisions of the clearly-visual (SR, 126, 157-62). Yet the passages which he discussed were not simply, or descriptively, visual, but metaphorical. Pound tried not wholly successfully to distinguish between what he saw as the 'suggestive' beauty of Shakespeare's 'Dawn in russet mantle clad' and Dante's more 'definite' beauty in extended comparisons like descriptions and similes, as well as his more compressed and elliptical metaphors. Accepting Aristotle's principle that the 'apt use of metaphor, arising, as it does, from a swift perception of relations, is the hallmark of genius', Pound then moved to distinguish a range of metaphor-like devices which work by both likeness and antithesis (SR, 158). In such tentative analysis, there lie the seeds of maturing aesthetic, and especially of his analysis of Imagism's Image.[35]

Pound's determination, after 1911, to modernise poetic diction led him to emphasise the importance of clarity, both visual and metaphorical. In his Imagist writings, he emphasised 'that sort of poetry which seems as if sculpture or painting were just forced or forcing itself into words' (LE, 380), and in *Cathay* (1915) and *Lustra* (1916) the poetry is the product of this new direction. After Amy Lowell 'stole' the Imagist movement and redirected it toward a looser free verse practice,[36]

Pound's own emphasis on the reform of diction for hardness, clarity and intensity grew (Letters, 79, 91-2) and he could use the very name, 'Imagisme',[37] in such a way as to associate it with the single principle of 'direct presentation' (LE, 380). Pound used terms like 'image', 'Imagisme', 'phanopoeia' rather loosely, and therefore a look at his sources and contexts seems necessary.

The origins of Pound's Imagist theory can probably be attributed to certain principles or discussions in the writings of Yeats, the British Bergsonian philosopher T E Hulme, and Remy de Gourmont. Yeats's description of symbolism as a mixture of the emotional and intellectual with an effect of transport[38] is echoed in Pound's definitions of the Image. On the other hand, Hulme like Pound himself found in Gourmont's book, *Le problème du style*, an emphasis on visual clarity and concrete literary presentation.[39] Hulme's attention to a relationship between visual imagery, metaphor, and linguistic precision appeared as early as 1909:

'Poetry . . . is not a counter language, but a visual concrete one. . . . It chooses fresh epithets and fresh metaphors not so much because they are new and we are tired of the old, but because the old cease to convey a physical thing and become abstract counters.'[40]

This material owes much to Gourmont's belief that initially the word is a pictorial entity which develops in the direction of abstraction, loses both its visual and its emotional values, and becomes merely a 'brass counter' or token.[41] Pound's Imagist definitions perhaps suffer from the confusions of his borrowings from authors and friends whose concerns were rather different.

In 'How to read' Pound defined a linguistic quality of 'phanopoeia' as 'a casting of images upon the visual imagination' (LE, 25). As a linguistic quality, this is resistant to technical definition, but phanopoeia must certainly be associated with the presentation of something objectively and concretely: this is the general weight of the concept which Pound presents. Normally, philosophers dealing with the problem of imagination and image-formation consider the role of memory. Pound however did not concern himself with analysing the status of the mental event; rather, he assumed that something happened, as a product of verbal precision, representational precision, and the operation of the *mot juste*. His Image was also strongly associated with emotion. Pound believed that intense emotion causes a pattern-unit, or unrepeated element of design, to *arise in the mind*, and this effect he also associated with the Image: it is not clear, in this case, that the Image is in any very important sense a representational event (SPr, 344-5).

The aims of Imagism include the phanopoeic function; but Imagist theory is more complex and inclusive than phanopoeic theory. There

77

is nothing in the Imagist manifesto, 'A few don'ts', which would be out of place in a general handbook of creative writing, and there is a good deal which is as properly applicable to prose as to poetry. In the section entitled 'Language' (LE, 4-7), Pound recommends a concise, concrete, self-critical use of diction, the study of models, and the use of enjambment and natural, spoken rhythms in verse.

Only the definition of the Image is in itself specialised: 'that which presents an intellectual and emotional complex in an instant of time' (LE, 4). Curiously, in the three principles of Imagisme which he listed in 'A Retrospect' (1918), the Image has vanished; the principles deal with directness of presentation, brevity, and the musical phrase, and there is no specific reference to an Image, or to any specifically visual quality (LE, 3). It is as though retrospectively Imagisme had become for Pound a public-relations exercise on behalf of modernism, concentrating on diction: simplification of syntax, concreteness, rhythmic freedom. Phanopeoia can only be linked with any ease to the first principle of the three: 'Direct treatment of the "thing" whether subjective or objective' — although the second ('no word that does not contribute to the presentation') might be seen as following from the first. But in phanopoeia there is 'the greatest drive toward utter precision of word' (LE, 26) and it is to be associated with 'concentration and pertinence'. Perhaps the Image was a kind of special case — that is, the specific means, any means, by which concentration and pertinence can be achieved, irrespective of form: merely the instrument of this purpose.

The Image, though phanopoeic in nature, was always something more than the simply pictorial or representational. As *something cast upon the imagination*, it must involve both mimetic and non-mimetic elements of meaning. For Pound, the true function of the Image was not simply to mirror the real world. At the same time, he was quite clear that it is not *symbolic* — it does not simply 'mean' something else.[41] Rather, in its mirroring of some aspect of reality, the aim is to create a flash of understanding in the reader's mind: an affective, psychological event. This is seen both in Pound's description of the Image as 'that which presents an intellectual and emotional complex in an instant of time' and in his addendum, a Pater-like comment that the effect of instantaneous presentation is the triggering, in the reader, of a sense of growth and liberation, always produced by great art (LE, 4). If we were to think of imagery as simply a mimetic event, then in emphasising its importance we would be laying an extreme value on the reproduction or mirroring of external reality by the poem. For Pound, the Image is rather an affective process causing a psychological event.

The essay 'Imagisme and England',[43] published in 1915, contains an attempt by Pound to discover a reputable ancestry for Imagisme in five centuries of English poetry and so provide his revolution with the

78

authority of tradition. Among the examples he offers there are three different kinds of Image, although Pound does not actually point this out. The first, Chaucer's *Prologue* portrait of the Wyf of Bath, is constructed by the accretion of descriptive details. Chaucer builds up a realistic picture by means of concrete contiguous elements, and produces the pictorial 'image' of popular usage. This is not a type of Image in Pound's own verse, nor did he deal with it in his criticism.[42] His second example is a single line by Lionel Johnson: 'Clear lie the fields, and fade into blue air.' Here the method of accretion is abandoned, and the effect of the line probably (for Pound does not stop to analyse it) depends on quite ordinary, pastoral connotations of the single words in context: 'clear', 'fields', 'blue air'. with the imaginative change of 'fade'; the diction is simple and clear, and the tone, elegaic. The third example, and that which Pound obviously most admired, is the thirty-one-line descriptive, subjective narration in Book I of Wordsworth's *Prelude*, of the child's theft of the rowing boat at night and his sense of being pursued by mountains, and something more than the physical, as he rows across the lake. Pound does not actually quote the passage, and in fact he refers to the poem as the 'Prologue', which suggests that he was working with some rather impressionistic criteria (and I suspect that this may also be true of the second example); it seems probable that these examples were chosen because of an emotional trace left in his memory. Certainly, considered as *visual* images, the three work very differently. All are concrete presentations (though the amount of detail given varies). All possess the directness and simplicity of diction associated with Pound's modernising Imagism. Chaucer's picture differs from the swift, vibrant line of Johnson as well as the emotionally subjectified narrative development of the event in the *Prelude*. Pound implied that the passages demonstrate the same quality; yet there are different degrees of objectification, and there is temporal development in the Johnson and the Wordsworth which are lacking in Chaucer's descriptive discourse with its achronological method. Pound's analysis is grossly incomplete. Possibly Wordsworth's passage most resembles a developed 'emotional and intellectual' complex, though the moment of time is necessarily extended; Johnson's *Cathay*-like line possesses both clarity and brevity, with the essential quality of a new creation of perception, a sudden awareness of the quiddity of the scene. Perhaps, for Pound, that same sudden awareness was a subjective effect of the Chaucerian passage? There is no way of knowing that.

What Pound seems to be implying is that the author's understanding and emotionally-based experience of some Thing is validated by his presentation of that Thing in an objective manner: by its being given a very clear, verbal authentification through being made co-terminous with a verifiable, human, sensuous experience: 'clear'/'blue'/'fade' is an

79

equation, or 'absolute metaphor' for a state of consciousness, a feeling of nostalgia and awe; and the looming mountain becomes an absolute metaphor for an awareness of transcendent spirit in physical nature, perceived in terror which is validated by an awareness of the unnatural movement, the blotting out of the light of the stars.

The pictorial associations in terms like 'image' and 'imagination', the emphasis on the need to modernise diction by making it concrete and clear, the attempt to find Imagism a genealogy in the English poetic tradition, and the cross-fertilisation of the concept of 'phanopoeia' — all these have merely added to the confusions about the nature of Pound's own Image in theory and practice. The reference in 'A few don'ts' to Hart and the 'psychological complex' (LE, 4) does suggest the truth, and an analysis of the poem which Pound offered as his own Imagist paradigm will also help to clarify things.

Bernard Hart defined the Freudian 'complex' as 'unconscious ideas . . . agglomerated into groups with accompanying effects, the systems thus formed being termed "complexes" '.[44] In 'The conception of the subconsious', Hart emphasised that the complex possesses an energy analogous to physical energy; it is this energy which appears in Pound's 1915 essay 'As for Imagisme', where the effect of sudden liberation, produced by the Image, is in the process of being accommodated to the new Vorticist theory (SPr, 344-47). Hart describes the complex as developed and manifested over a period of time. Pound scholars have tended to follow Pound's own reference to the 'instant of time'; but the slower development accords both with the Chaucerian and Wordsworthian examples we have seen very clearly, and there is an element of change, of fading, which is at the centre of the effect of Johnson's single line.

In *Gaudier-Brzeska* (1916), Pound presented his own two-line poem, 'In a station of the Metro', as the exemplary Imagist verse (GB, 100-3). This poem does have strongly visual elements; and the account which Pound gives of the genesis of the poem is in terms of a visual experience, although it might be worth pointing out that the typography used for the original printing relates those elements emphatically to sound-phrasing, as they are gathered into two clusters:

> 'The apparition   of these faces   in the crowd:
> Petals   on a wet, black   bough.'   (CSP, 119)[45]

The spaces within the lines tend to emphasise a sequential appearance of details making up two concrete visual perceptions, each with a different set of natural associations; the spaces control the reader's attention as it moves from detail to detail, and the pauses give some additional time for the associations to develop independently. The poem is basically asyntactical communication. The two lines are related to one another

80

by a partly-parallel word order, but the relationship is not given an interpretation by means of syntax. The words refer very simply and closely to a sequence of things; but their total meaning is produced by their contiguity. In his description of the poem, Pound referred to the 'super-position' of two elements (GB, 103) and because of this readers have tended to think in terms of a metaphorical juxtaposition. However it is perfectly clear that the two elements *do not fuse and become one* at any point; they are related to one another by their objective contiguity, but the point of the poem is lost if the reader does not remain aware of their separateness. The faces and the petals are *not* completely super-posed, and the term 'apparition' reinforces the movement of attention, and ensures that we remain aware of both similarity and dissimilarity. The strategy is one of contiguity, or metonymy;[46] the visual analogy is to the art of collage.

'In a station of the Metro' works, then, rather like the Japanese *haiku*[47] form which it imitates, its meaning cohering in the instantaneous perception of *discordia concors*, the true nature of the thing. In describing the genesis of the poem as an attempt to express a visual impression by juxtaposing two objective 'ideas' (the use of the conceptual term is confusing, but has at least the advantage of directing attention to other than visual matters) Pound wrote:

'In a poem of this sort one is trying to record the precise instant when a thing outward and objective transforms itself, or darts into a thing inward and subjective.' (GB, 103)

Most of his Imagist poems are more extensive in their development of their complex. In 'April' (CSP, 101), 'Gentildonna' (CSP, 101), 'Alba' (CSP, 119) and 'L'art 1910' (CSP, 124) the intensive Image is combined with less concrete passages of description; 'Fan piece' (CSP, 118) and (at another extreme of tone) 'The bath tub' (CSP, 109) preserve something of the elliptical contiguity of the simple *haiku* form. The one-line Image which focuses the meaning of a preceding passage in a single, vivid, accretive stroke is something which Pound uses repeatedly in longer poems including the *Cantos*, where it may often be found in the form of a single strikingly descriptive line, logically unconnected with the preceding passage, yet so placed as to analogise it:

'And the castelan of Montefiori wrote down,
"You'd better keep him out of the district.
"When he got back here from Sparta, the people
"Lit fires, and turned out yelling, 'PANDOLFO!'" '
In the gloom, the gold gathers the light against it.' (Canto 11/51)

This gives us the moment of manifestation of a complex, the moment of its affect.

Pound distinguished two varieties of Imagism in his own work: poems like 'The return' (CSP, 85) which demonstrate visual qualities in presenting objective reality, and those like 'Heather' (CSP, 119) which 'imply' a subjective state of consciousness rather than an objective reality (GB, 98). The visual clarity of 'Heather' resembles the static quality of much of *Cathay*; the Image of 'The return' owes more to its cadences and irregular rhythms than to visual qualities. But in both, as Pound reminded his readers, 'the natural object is always the *adequate* symbol' (LE, 5), for the direct presentation of the object triggers the perception of the 'thing' in sensuous and emotional terms. Similarly, poems like 'A game of chess', 'Phanopoeia' and 'Albatre' (CSP, 187-8) although they consist entirely of arrangements of colours and named objects, are not word-pictures, but arrangements analogous to the arrangements of planes and colours in a painting by Whistler. Imagism is opposed to the mimetic word-picture, which should be thought of as an impressionist technique: Pound associated impressionism with imprecision, linguistic laxity, and the unenergetic accretiveness of prose, for in an essay on Joyce, he mused that even the best impressionists of language are often 'so intent on exact presentation' that they neglect intensity (LE, 399-400). Therefore he rejected any attempt to 'imitate in words what someone has done in paint'.

Imagism belongs to poetry and no other medium. Its development was the rejection of conceptualisation (which abstracts) and descriptive narration (which builds a novel mirroring aspects of the 'real world' by a process of addition rather than of intensive contiguities); it uses a language which will 'hover above and cling' to the physical and emotional reality it signifies (SPr, 29). As Pound began, after a few months, to assimilate his Imagist theory to the new Vorticist movement, he wrote of the Image in ways which focus more on its energising force than on any visual power: it is a cluster endowed with energy; it is ideas embodied in the energy of related things (SPr, 345); it is the objectification of a mode of thought. What all this amounts to is the shadowy perception of a linguistic system in which the verbal sign and the signified concept are so closely and naturally related that the reader's reading is comprehensive, perceptive, and objectively true.

Much of the problem, for readers of Pound's criticism, is that he did not possess and could not invent a set of critical terms which could carry his theory in a rigorously consistent manner. As a result, his Imagist theory remains confused and paradoxical, full of unresolved dualisms. It is possible to gather that his impulse toward the reform of diction was based on a perception of the nature of language, and that what Pound proposed was a peculiarly literary form of discourse in which the signifying power of the word was very direct and unarbitrary, while its energy derived from aspects of word-order — aspects of which a connotative juxtaposition and, in verse syllabic relationships were prominent, and the structuring of normal English syntax (subject, verb, object) becomes unimportant. Contiguity and syllabic relationship were, I think, the means of producing absolute metaphor and absolute rhythm, respectively. Imagist theorising, and the concept of the Image at its fullest stretch, dealt with the act of communication, hence the rather confusing references to the Image as an 'idea' or cluster of ideas. It is closer to a symbol in the directness of its communication of thought and feeling, but the Image unlike the symbol objectifies the whole communicated meaning, and lacks the mysterious open-endedness of the true poetic symbol. In fact, this 'intellectual and emotional complex' is above all the formal manifestation of a psychological experience. It is the culmination, in Pound's theory, of his old search for the Longinian sublime and its thunderbolt effect, it is the fragment which bursts suddenly upon the amazed perception. It can be seen as both poetic diction and a trigger: both a sign in a coded system of signification, and an emotional catalyst:

'Poetry is a centaur. The thinking word-arranging, clarifying faculty, must move and leap with the energizing, sentient, musical faculties.' (LE, 52)
'An "Image" is that which presents an intellectual and emotional complex in an instant of time.' (LE, 4)
'Energy, or emotion, expresses itself in form. . . . When an energy or emotion "presents an image", this may find adequate expression in words.' (SPr, 346)

Therefore the Image can be seen as a relationship, or as the visible middle term of the invisible psychological equation between object and subject, between the poet's experience and the reader's. The poet remains outside the poem, nor is the experience contaminated by the reader; there is no space for formal conventions in the Image, and therefore no convention can distort the directness of the equation, either its expression or its effect. But the emotional charge which intensifies language has 'come upon' the intellect of the reader and fused with it, forming a new mode of experience, a new subject, while itself remaining objectively the same, the words on the page.

There is nothing very original about Pound's theory, which springs from the old Longinian tradition of ecstasy, transport, and includes the principle of the immediate intuitive apprehension of knowledge which was discussed by Thomas de Quincy, another of Pound's early theoretical masters (SR, 158). The references to the 'complex' gives to tradition the support of an aggressively modern, and apparently scientific, authority. In fact, his attempt to consider poetry as a linguistic construct was by far the more modern aspect of his theory, however confused its practice.

83

Vorticism and the problem of form

Melopoeia and phanopoeia, with the associated Image, and Imagism, provided a schematology for poetic discourse: intensity, energy. The creative and propagandising efforts associated with them, culminating in the quarrels of the Imagist movement, have led students and scholars to feel that these were the most problematic, most important elements of Pound's theory. Pound also described a third kind of verbal energy in 'Logopoeia'. This type is more difficult to define and trace — more 'slippery' as Pound admitted (LE, 25), which may be why it seems to have aroused less interest and controversy. Together, these provide a way of looking at poetry as *language*. But Pound was seeking an inclusive system to account for poetry, and this he added not by means of a further subdivision of linguistic usage, but by outer forms: 'All writing is made up of these three elements plus "architectonics" or "the form of the whole". (LE, 26) To add a category of form to the linguistic categories might be seen as a failure of nerve, a lack of awareness of the full implications of his theory; for linguistic categories and formal categories imply very different and rather contradictory views of the nature of literature.

Recognising that Pound's aesthetic of form originated, as with so much of his thinking, in the Romantic-expressionist ideas of his earliest years, it can be admitted that what he wrote about form was inconsistent, largely because of his failure to develop a consistent critical terminology. For example, in the Vorticist book, *Gaudier-Brzeska: a memoir* (1916), the work which gathers together much of Pound's most persistent writing about form, there is one page on which he can be found using the word with three quite different implied meanings (GB, 93).

Basically, there are two ways of looking at form in art, and Pound used both ways. This inconsistency too may have stemmed from his early model, Dante. *De vulgari eloquentia* refers to the physical and conventional poetic shape of stanza, rhyme scheme and metre as its 'form' — the most popular usage. Pound at first thought of form and meaning as separable; in an early letter he told his mother that a 'thing' which is insufficiently interesting to be 'put' into verse is not worth writing,[48] and a doggerel verse dating from 1907 supports this:

> ' . . . We make the yolk philosophy
> True beauty the albumen
> & then glue on a shell of form
> to make the screed sound human.'[49]

This usage hides the assumption that the 'meaning' of a poem exists in the poet's mind before it is expressed in a form which allows it to be communicated. This kind of form must be seen as mimetic. It must

84

represent the thing to be communicated. Furthermore, it is socially and historically determined so that systems of rules are developed; the 'eggshell' of Pound's statement with its social and normalising function must pertain to 'appropriate' kinds of expression, given the nature of that pre-existing concept, or blueprint of meaning. Much classical and neo-classical theory follows this line of thought. Thus, poetic tragedy comes to seem the form appropriate to the representation of the fall of great men; the sonnet, the form appropriate to a certain kind of love poem with a twist in the sestet-tail; unrhymed iambic pentameter, the form appropriate to the English epic. Examples are easy to multiply, and produce a range, from a theory of genres to familiar neo-classical rules about metre, stanza forms, and decorum in general. *De vulgari eloquentia* is based on this kind of description of poetic forms.

However, during the same period Pound saw in *De vulgari eloquentia* a message about the organic nature of poetry, a text in which sound and sense cohere.[50] From Dante, and perhaps others like Coleridge in the Romantic tradition, he took the concept of poetry as a unified and self-dependent product of the author's *virtù* – the energies of his unique emotional energy, his creative imagination, the organising force which holds in tension the materials of the poetic text (SPr, 28-31, 34). The 'Osiris' essays view intellectual energy as both a *formal* power and a source of aesthetic pleasure. Following the hint of Coleridge's *to kalon*, (CSP, 105; SR, 149) he equated order with beauty; and the equation survived into the *Cantos* in a thematic assertion of a relationship between beauty and order, art and life.

By 1918, Pound had accommodated the dualism of his old ideas by distinguishing two types of form:

'I think there is a "fluid" as well as a "solid" content, that some poems may have form as a tree has form, some as water poured into a vase. That most symmetrical forms have certain uses. That a vast number of subjects cannot be precisely, and therefore not properly rendered in symmetrical forms.'
' "Thinking that alone worthy wherein the whole art is employed" (Dante, *De volgari eloquio*). I think the artist should master all known forms and systems of metric. . . .' (LE, 9)

'A Retrospect' thus acknowledges both the conventional forms, where meaning exists in the artist's intentions and is 'poured' into a pre-determined line, stanza-shape, or genre; and a view of form as the direct, unique expression of material, an expression of emotional and intellectual energy, like a magnetic field.

Much of Pound's earliest poetry and translation worked within the boundaries of a poetry written by shaping materials in accordance with various established formal conventions. Much of his pre-1912 verse can be seen as a struggle to control and vary such forms and expand their communicative possibilities. However, 'solid content' (to quote Pound's rather uninformative term) possesses inherent form — perhaps an absolute form, by analogy with absolute rhythm and absolute metaphor. Form is a function of meaning. From 1912 onward, Pound's main interest was in such abstract, absolute formalism; this is another of the threads of theory which he wove into Imagism, and a consequence of the melopoeic impulse to free verse, 'where presumably, the nature of the thing expressed or of the person supposed to be expressing it, is antagonistic to external symmetry. Form may delight by its symmetry or by its aptness.' (SPr, 330) His formal theorising reached a climax during the years between 1912 and 1920, particularly in relation to Vorticism's 'point of maximum energy' (GB, 93) and 'renewal of the sense of construction'.[52]

The movement called Vorticism, which centred in Wyndham Lewis's Rebel Art Centre and the two issues of BLAST, meant different things to different participants.[53] For Wyndham Lewis it involved a destructive energy not (in spite of contemporary feuds and possibly a stronger element of craftsmanship) in theory so very different from Futurism;[54] for Hueffer, it was perhaps a fad; for Gaudier-Brzeska and other BLAST contributors, a kind of family joke.[55] but in terms of strategy it was at least two things for Pound: the opportunity to forward an aesthetic Renaissance based on poetry and the fine arts, and the related chance to place his concept of Imagism in an inclusive aesthetic which could simultaneously accommodate both the expressive and the objective:

'Our respect is not for the subject-matter, but for the creative power of the artist; for that which he is capable of adding to his subject from himself; or in fact his capacity to dispense with external subject altogether. . . . ' (GB, 114)

Since the time of the 'Osiris' essays of 1911-12, Pound had been seeking to establish a cultural and artistic Renaissance defined as a social 'vortex' — the energy of tradition and race-consciousness (S Pr, 34). Pound claimed to have given Vorticism its name. The social connotation of the term may be found in Thomas de Quincey's essay, 'Style', where he envisaged a cultural phenomenon which may well, since de Quincey was one of Pound's earliest acknowledged critical influences, have influenced this sense of Pound's terminology and approach:

'This contagion of sympathy runs electrically through society, searches high and low for congenital powers, and suffers none to lurk unknown to its possessor. A vortex is created which draws into its suction whatever is liable to a similar action.'[56]

86

The term 'vortex', in its second and related sense of a shaping energy, appeared in Pound's writings in the 1908 poem, 'Plotinus' (ALS, 56) and was therefore available to subsume the individual *virtù* of Pound's early theory into the collaborative, cultural model of Vorticism.

Pound's version of Vorticism is outlined in the essays 'Vortex' and 'Chronicles' in the two issues of BLAST; in 'Vorticism', published in September 1914; 'Affirmations', a series of essays for *The new age* in 1915; and the book *Gaudier-Brzeska: a memoir* (1916) which republishes some of the earlier material. They are very eclectic arguments, for some of the ideas go back to James McNeill Whistler's 'Ten o'clock lecture' (GB, 146-51) — a work which Pound knew and admired even before he left America. Pound bundled Imagism into his version of Vorticism — indeed at the time he may have regarded the distinction as accidental, a change of personnel rather than aesthetic.[57] But the essential part of Vorticism, in its theoretical rather than its social aspect, was the retrieval of the energy which he felt that Amy Lowell's looser form of Imagism had betrayed (Letters, 122) and the simultaneous and associated rejection of mimesis. The Image, as we have seen it, tended to place two representational elements in a non-representational contiguity. Pound specifically denied that the Image was metonymic (GB, 84) therefore the elements must be regarded as *more than* merely contiguous; or alternatively we must suspect that Vorticism had infected the way in which Pound thought of the original Image. Now, returning to energy (or *virtù*), Pound began to emphasise active energy, 'the "light of the DOER, as it were a form clearing to it" means an ACTIVE pattern, a pattern that sets things in motion.'[58] The Image, that 'radiant node or cluster' was re-defined as the vortex, 'from which, and through which, and into which, ideas are constantly rushing'. (S Pr, 345) If Pound sometimes seemed to suggest that Imagism and Vorticism were the same, or that the former was merely the poetic sub-division of the latter, this is misleading:

'Every concept, every emotion presents itself to the vivid consciousness in some primary form. It belongs to the art of this form. If sound, to music; if formed words, to literature; the image, to poetry; form, to design; colour in position, to painting; form or design in three planes, to sculpture; movement, to the dance or to the rhythm of music or verse.' (GB, 93)

But this 'primary pigment' theory tends to obscure the fact that the Image seems more static, more deliberate, than the pure energy, or confluence of forces, in the vortex. It might be more accurate to see the Image as a function of precise diction, and Vorticism as representing an additional pattern-making, formal element which is more abstract in the way we perceive it than any representational form can be. This is

87

the reason why, writing about the vortex, Pound moved away from a terminology which deals with objects toward one of forces and energies. Pattern becomes the product of creative energy; perhaps the vortex should be described, not as a visible pattern, but as the abstract potential for a pattern, or form.

This becomes clearer if we consider Pound's statements about the visual arts, especially painting. In BLAST, Pound acknowledged his debt to Whistler and to Laurence Binyon for the idea of a painting and sculpture which is *a series of spatial relations ordered by the artist's will into a single statement* (GB, 167-8). Whistler had been adopted by Vorticism as part of a strategy against narrative and mimesis (GB, 98ff). Bad art occurs when the elements of expression — mass, colour — are isolated and lack the relationship of a connecting energy. This isolation and de-energisation is what Pound, in *Gaudier-Brzeska*, calls 'impressionism', applying the word here to painting, but elsewhere as well, by analogy, to literature (LE, 399-400) and music (LE, 433-4). In discussing Wyndham Lewis's pictures, Pound emphasised the value of the self-consistent, self-referring, 'natural' arrangement of masses and planes in relationships which express emotion and meaning completely: so that the work is an organic, whole object like any object in nature,[59] or indeed like a poem. No Vorticist work can possess an idea or meaning which is separable from form (LE, 441), and form — being the expression of the artist's energy — is a non-verbal quality expressing non-verbal meanings, and cannot be meaningless itself though it is never representational. The work of art stands on the plane of physical reality. It is an autonomous phenomenon; or in the words which Pound quoted, in capital letters, from Binyon's *The flight of the dragon*: 'FOR INDEED IT IS NOT ESSENTIAL THAT THE SUBJECT MATTER SHOULD REPRESENT OR BE LIKE ANYTHING IN NATURE: ONLY IT MUST BE ALIVE WITH A RHYTHMIC VITALITY OF ITS OWN.' (GB, 168). It is in this sense and this context that Pound would quote Walter Pater's famous tag, that 'All arts approach the condition of music' (GB, 146).

It was characteristic of the Vorticist period that Pound wrote of physical energy which functions to shape the flux of experience into meaningfulness. Thus 'organisation of forms' became his description of the aesthetic object; and this organisation itself expresses the poet's power, just as diction expresses the conceptual and emotional significance of the successive elements of the poem. Pound was trying at this point to support his perceptions by means of modern scientific analogies, so he compared the formative energy to the energy of a magnetic field. Magnetic energy organises form in a way which is made perceptible by a plate of iron filings; it brings order and therefore beauty into something which, in its isolated elements, had been ugly

88

and of course meaningless. 'The design in the magnetised iron filings expresses a confluence of energy. It is not "meaningless" or "inexpressive".'[60] This is the image of the rose in the steel dust, which recurs in Pound's later writings and became the almost-mystical symbol objectifying his ideal of form and beauty.[61] The energy itself is invisible and inaudible, so that the sensuous aspects of language cannot express it, only its symptoms are perceived in the abstractions of relationship, or form.

The vortex is innate form, form as an abstraction perceived in the concreteness of art. The iron filings are an evidence of energy; they make not it, but the fact of its presence, visible. Words are visible, audible proof of the presence of energy; the energy is not in the single word, but in relationship itself: in *pattern*. Vorticism is the awareness of a unique, unrepeated pattern-unit which is specifically and innately non-representational (LE, 441).

A simple illustration of poetic Vorticism can be seen in a text like 'The game of chess', in which movement and relationship are presented as the content of the poem:

'Red knights, brown bishops, bright queens,
Striking the board, falling in strong 'L's of colour.
Reaching and striking in angles,
      holding lines in one colour.
This board is alive with light;
      these pieces are living in form.
Their moves break and reform the pattern:
      luminous green from the rooks,
Clashing with "X"s of queens,
      looped with the knight-leaps.

' "Y" pawns, clearing, embanking!
Whirl! Centripetal! Mate! King down in the
      vortex,
Clash, leaping of bands, straight strips of hard
      colour,
Blocked lights working in. Escapes. Renewal of
      contest.'   (CSP, 131)

Despite the warning reference to the vortex, the poem is not entirely consistent in Vorticist terms. The statement of the fifth and sixth lines is a descriptive assertion which ought to be presented by pattern and relationship, objectively. Possibly also the static and assertive verb 'is' is also inherently unVorticist. Elsewhere, however, the movement of elements in relationship is a more purely energetic design, and the second stanza (except for the interpretative word 'Mate!' in the third line) more clearly provides a non-representational presentation of a non-discursive experience in its 'undending adventure towards "arrangement", this search for the equations of eternity' (GB, 148).

The fact that a poem like this presents colours and movements directly, in abstract pattern-elements, suggests Pound's search for a common ground for the arts, a general aesthetic which would comprehend all modes of expression. His idea of a primary pigment or medium proper to each individual art form allows for different forms of expression, all operating by the same principle of relationships, but each appropriate to a different type of perception, each the most energised:

> 'THE PRIMARY PIGMENT
> The vorticist relies on this alone . . .
> Every concept,   every emotion presents itself to the vivid consciousness in some primary form.
> 'It is the picture that means a hundred poems, the music that means a hundred pictures, the most highly energised statement, the statement that has not yet SPENT itself in expression, but which is the most capable of expressing.'[62]

The emphasis on energy is Pound's, and Vorticism's, although once more Pound was borrowing the theory in part from Walter Pater, whose book *The Renaissance* Pound appears to have re-read at about this time: for in the beginning of the essay on 'The school of Giorgione', Pater discusses the distinct sensuous inputs into painting, music and poetry, and goes on to suggest the fusion of form and content in a section on colour and line in patterns, and propose an analogy with poetry. Thus Pater was proposing something like the primary pigment concept as specific means of communicating with the imaginative powers of an audience.[63] This distinction separates the different media, but reveals a common purpose and energy. So Pound follows Pater into a system which simultaneously connects and separates the arts, rejecting word-painting for the Image, and moving away from representation. 'Vorticism means that one is interested in the creative faculty as opposed to the mimetic.'[64] 'Our respect is not for the subject matter, but for the creative power of the artist: . . . his capability to dispense with external subjects altogether. . . .' (GB, 114) Much of Vorticist theory is clearly foreshadowed in the *virtù* doctrine of the 'Osiris' essays.

It might be worth pointing out that Pound may have considered prose form as different from that of other arts. While Pound claimed for example to detect in the work of Henry James 'titanic volume, weight, in the masses which he sets in opposition within his work' (LE, 297; 333-6), he normally perceived the novel as linearly shaped by the addition of details and detailed impressions, so that it achieves its power by the weight of accretion, of 'so arranging the circumstances that some perfectly simple speech, perception, dogmatic statement

90

appears in abnormal vigour' (LE, 324n). Prose is seen here as additive, massive and mimetic, with a role for descriptive discourse and narrative (mimesis including action); whereas poetry is selective and abstract. But Pound made few clear statements about prose form. I suspect that the idea defeated him, for his criteria for the novels he reviewed tended to be social, and to relate to authenticity and a satirical purpose. Detail in prose is a function of the major form which, in a play or novel, includes the action of the work and is therefore chronological and causal. His reviews normally dwell on plot outlines and characters, and these (to his way of thinking) tend to block other kinds of contiguity, and poetic intensity. Because of the cumulative structure of narrative, its imposed Aristotelian form of beginning, middle and end — the symmetrical or 'fluid' kind of form — is essential to control textual detail.[66] Therefore, although Pound described the correspondences of Joyce's *Ulysses* as a triumph of 'form', he also rejected the fecund observed detail as 'impressionism', the failure to attain a total energetic relationship between the disparate moments of sharp observation (LE, 406). In mentioning an 'element of form' which does not govern the whole book, but affects certain chapters (LE, 397) Pound excludes the narrative from the category of solid form in the old distinction, but allows for an Image set within discursive narrative, the temporary and rapid synthesis of detail, the energetic relation of elements achieving a formal unity independent of the rest of the book.

In poetic theory, on the other hand, Pound accommodated his early expressionist beliefs to later formalist assumptions by seeing the poem, like its 'primary pigment' of Image, as the product of the creative imagination, or *virtù*, which conceives rather than merely reflecting reality.[67] Narrative discourse, being causal and temporal, reflects reality but is not reality itself. On the other hand, the *unrepeated* pattern-unit of Vorticist form is vital, unique, and absolute; it does not mirror the physical world, but communicates energy, form and relationship very directly.[68] The status of that communication must be considered.

In his slightly uneasy, sometimes uncertain (GB, 99) shift away from representation, Pound's Vorticism attained a different emphasis from either Gaudier's increasing naturalism or Wyndham Lewis's: it was concerned with 'form, not the *form of anything*' (GB, 115). With a growing emphasis on form as the expression of energy, much of what Pound wrote about form after 1915 was affective, for he postulated a psychological event in the mind of the reader, an event of which the Vorticist work is a catalyst. The sculptor's form is 'cast' by its arrangement of planes; the poetic Image is 'cast' upon the mind by an arrangement of words. Poetic diction is not seen as an 'arrangement of names'; the word has become a 'name', although Pound does not emphasise its function as an abstracter of reality, a code or concept, instead he tends

91

to write about it affectively: 'An *image*, in our sense, is real because we know it directly' (GB, 99), and it 'casts a more definite image' than other, unformed communications (GB, 147). The purpose, Pound agreed, was to 'give people new eyes' (GB, 98). Words are the things which the poet arranges in the way that the fine artist handles the planes and colours of the visual arts, or the musician, musical notes. Their meaning is in their intensive relationships and is achieved by order and juxta-position, in the space between the words. Explaining the apparent logical impossibility of his notion of unrepeated units of pattern, Pound referred to a poet expressing his meaning in words,

' . . . by mentioning them close together or by using some device or simile or metaphor that is a legitimate procedure of his art, but with the names of objects and their properties. It is his business to use, so to arrange, these names as to cause a more definite image than the layman can cast. . . . This is the common ground of the arts, this combat of arrangements or "harmony".' (GB, 147)[68]

In other words, form, meaning and affect are all the products of the specific utterance of the work in relation to the general verbal code of which it makes use. The special arrangement or juxtaposition of ele-ments in each text or utterance creates an Image, which exists in *form*, in the vital relationship of elements. The unrepeated unit of pattern *is* the poem, and each poem is in a real sense a unique, new language, an unrepeatable usage within the general discourse of poetry.

Now, in all essentials this is a description of the Ideogram,[69] which is Pound's ultimate principle of absolute form, functioning in the tem-porary and instantaneous synthesis of detail: a relationship. The ideo-gram functions in the world of experience because it affects perception, educates the faculties of understanding, and creates a new subject in the real world. It is the culmination of all Pound's musical and visual analogies, and his urge to reform poetic diction. Pound never wholly abandoned 'architectonic form' in literature as a concept; nor did he apparently recognise that the ideogram had made it redundant. However, his late rejection of Aristotelian logic was in effect a rejection of 'form', and by 1928 he was questioning the need for form in the old sense, even in epic, drama and the novel (LE, 394). Form itself, in the usual sense, had vanished from the essence of art; but form in its new and non-mimetic sense had become the basis of meaning itself.

IV

KNOWLEDGE AND THE *CANTOS*

Logopoeia
TWO of the energisers of poetic language — melopoeia and phanopoeia
— were related to sensory qualities. Pound's third 'energy' was not:

'LOGOPOEIA, "the dance of the intellect among words", that is to
say, it employs words not only for their direct meaning, but it takes
count in a special way of habits of usage, of the contexts we *expect* to
find with the word, its usual concomitants, of its known acceptances,
and of ironical play. It holds the aesthetic content which is peculiarly
the domain of verbal manifestation and cannot possibly be contained in
plastic or in music. It is the latest come, and perhaps the most tricky
and undependable mode.' (LE, 25; cp. ABC, 36)

Logopoeia is not merely a connotative mode, like the others, but it
is *contextual* as well as *intertextual*. In Imagism, Pound had worked to
strip words of old associations and create new and unique ones: the
faces in the crowd and the petals on the bough are pulled out of their
normal contexts, and their strange juxtaposition creates a sharp and
immediate context for a new emotional and perceptual contiguity.
Immediacy is essential to the Image — the record of a moment of
perceptual experience brought about by stripping words of their
historically-developed contexts. Melopoeia — seen as the unique equation
for the emotional import — and phanopeia are, both, the objectifications
of intellectual and emotional perception. They are expressive and
experimental. They are also self-contained, and therefore wholly open
to the critical formalist: to the reading of the text on the page. Logopoeia is innately different.
Logopoeia is a metalinguistic category. It is language which carries
its history with it and depends on the reader's recognition of that
burden. With logopoeia, Pound assumed that the reader is capable of an
act of recognition based on knowledge of rhetorical usage, and therefore requiring a considerable measure of educated reading experience.
Logopoeic significance is derived, not from the sensory and objective
elements, but from language alone, from usages viewed conceptually
and in many cases, as Pound's listings of logopoeic writers suggests,

93

ironically: Rochester, Dorset, Heine, and above all Propertius and Laforgue (LE, 33). Of course all poems are in some sense written in the context of the body of poetry which already exists, and Pound's literary traditionalism had always been a recognition of the fact.[1] But in 'logopoeia' he was naming a linguistic usage which recognises this intertextuality. The *language* of the poem is to be read in relation to previous usages.

Although he presented logopoeia as though it too were an objective usage (for after all, it does refer to pre-existing patterns, merely altering these in a way which carries meaning; and such patterns are objectively available to the reader or student), in fact this is a very subjective mode. Its success depends on the intellectual powers of the writer, including his habits and accidents of recollection and association. Pound acknowledged that this was 'tricky and undependable'. Successful communication of meaning depends here on the skill and awareness with which the writer attends to the intellectual habits, the reading habits, of his specific audience. Success implies a reliance on expectations arising from previous literary experience.[2]

From about 1915, Pound was very consious of language as a cultural system which is the product of past usage, 'with roots, with associations, with how and where the word is familiarly used, or where it has been used brilliantly or memorably' (ABC, 36). From the Vorticist period onward, his writings make much of intelligence, both as a critical, cultural power and as a motive force for art, replacing emotion: 'Art comes from intellects stirred by will, impulse, emotion, but art is emphatically not any of these others deprived of intellect. . .' (GB, 125). Poetry's heuristic function, according to Pound, is to focus the mind on definitions, to sharpen 'verbal apperceptions'.[3] Satire, irony and deliberate ambiguity become instruments of an élite intellect in revolt against the stupidity of the mass culture. And Pound set about discovering or defining a tradition, from Propertius to Voltaire to Gourmont, Lewis, Joyce, Eliot and himself, of those writers who have used the weapon of their intellect to 'drive' intelligence into society in an act of social reform.[4]

It is easy to assume that Pound somehow changed directions because of his involvement with Vorticism, or his discovery of Gourmont. Yet his early interest in Latin satire and the 'luminous' intelligence of Dante[5] foreshadows logopoeia; so does the 'Osiris' essay 'On technique', with its reference to the precision which results when the right conjunction of the right words makes language augment itself and produce a verbally-based energy which 'is the power of tradition, of centuries of race consciousness, of agreement, of association; and the control of it is the "Technique of content" . . .' (S Pr, 34). When Pound discovered intelligence and verbal hardness in the work of Tailhade, Gautier and

94

Laforgue,[5] he already had a place for them in his theory. However it was Laforgue's work which specifically helped Pound to focus on the nature of his own discovery, when he identified the 'verbalism' of logopoeia – a verbal play which exploits multiple meanings in conventional phrases.[6] Tone and allusion are the basis of this verbalism: allusive use of materials from many sources, of ironic clichés, of the Latinate diction associated with social satire, of mock grandeur and mock pedantry and the deliberate use of anachronistic materials. Laforgue's 'verbalism' was the beginning of Pound's understanding of the logopoeic quality:

'... he is most "verbalist". Bad verbalism is rhetoric, or the use of cliché unconsciously, or a mere playing with phrases. But there is good verbalism, distinct from lyricism or imagism ... an international tongue common to the excessively cultivated.... Verbalism demands a set form used with irreproachable skill. Satire needs, usually, the form of cutting rhymes to drive it home.' (LE, 282)

The reference to the 'international tongue' is problematic, for the verbalism of logopoeia depends on a linguistic heritage and is therefore culturally limited – at least it 'does not translate' (LE, 25), although insofar as it is the expression of an attitude or mental 'tone' an equivalent may be found in another culture. The fact is that Pound believed he had perceived the quality in the writings of several times and places and languages, and that the quality is a recurring product of a type of allusive intelligence which focused itself critically upon its contemporary cultural context (LE, 418-9).[6] It is clear that he believed he had found logopoeia in the *Elegies* of Propertius, and also that he had translated it by using comparable logopoeic devices in English: allusions from various literary sources, the ironic clichés which dot his *Homage to Sextus Propertius*, the Latinate diction, the mock pedantry communicated by stilted translatorese phrases, the anachronistic references to policemen and refrigerators, and so on.

Pound's purpose in the *Homage* is clear enough if we look at the work in relation to what he said about Laforgue and T S Eliot. Whether he achieved his aims is another matter; it took critics quite a few years to accept that they understood what Pound was about.[7] One of the signs which he had offered them was in the deliberate mistranslations of the 'devirginated' young ladies and the 'frigidaire patent'; another was the deliberate pointing of tone in the second poem, where 'public' verse is 'yawned out', so that where the original promised a state epic, Pound derives from its tone a rather different intention; and another is most clearly to be seen in the creaking syntax of the clumsy translator: 'Me happy, night, night full of brightness. . . .' (CSP 237) where English poetic diction plays between colloquial control and the apparently-

95

helpless collapse into the stiffness of fourth-rate, second-hand, literal-translation verse. Play with tone is clearly intended to convey more about the 'whole situation' of a poet, or of The Poet, than is simply denoted by either the content of the original elegies, or the 'translation' of them: 'homage' lies in the observation of character, signified by a quality of the discourse in relation to the individual words, more than any content.

It is in this area of logopoeic diction, of associations that work like signifiers, that *Propertius* differs from the early *persona* poems. Those were more creative than critical, despite their literary references, because they recreated characters, with Pound's own personality self-consciously repressed and a certain unspoken criterion of authenticity at work.[8] The centre of logopoeia in the *Homage* lies between the original Propertian texts and Pound seeing-through Propertius. The reader is not intended to see the *Elegies*, but a new poem with a rhetorical relationship to them, which is a 'derivative or equivalent' of Propertius's (LE, 25).

Pound's acceptance that logopeia cannot be literally translated may well have been the product of hind-sight, fuelled by classicists' attacks on his *Propertius*. But it is reasonable to question the possibility, in a method so dependent on linguistic context and usage, of translating logopoeic qualities without a special awareness of the differences in those usages between one language, culture and literary tradition, and the other. The *fact* of an ironical tone, verbal ambiguities and social observations may be translated into other terms, as the *Homage* reveals. Had Pound written a critical description of such qualities in the *Elegies*, his task would have been more comprehensible. A logopoeic demonstration without a descriptive framework is, however, a renewal *in addition to* a demonstration, and it was this renewal which Pound wished, desiring to import into modern English poetry 'a language that was not the stilted Horatian peg-work or Georgian maunder of Maro'.[9] The irony, he attempted to translate by means of a mixture of Latinate English and journalese, of high literary and low colloquial diction. This is used to communicate what Pound saw as criticism of a social situation having much in common with his own; therefore it comments obliquely on the jingoistic and provincial mental habits, attitudes and motives which Pound associated with wartime cultures. The *Homage* was written in 1917; it is a complex and ambiguous assertion of private and aesthetic values. Pound selected his material and slanted his language in order to emphasise what he understood to be Propertius's beliefs and aesthetic intention; Propertius's attitudes are grasped indirectly rather than discursively, by the comparative method in the logopoeic context.

Propertius is one kind of approach to the mystery of the historical document and the question of the extent to which any statement it

96

makes is 'true'. In the terms of 'Date line', the *Homage* is an act of literary criticism on the linguistic plane. Or in other words, the nature of Pound's 'translation' from Latin into modern English indicates the translator's view of the connotative meanings of the original, in this case by clearly-marked, self-consciously ironical tone. It asserts two levels of relevance. On the first, Pound affirms the appropriateness of Propertian attitudes to modern society, and specifically to its literary establishment. On the second, he asserts by demonstration that Propertian logopoeia expresses that appropriateness. A self-mocking irony provides the mental tone of the poets thus juxtaposed — the apparent author, Propertius, and the hidden author but apparent translator, Pound, who is the actual author in the sense of providing the authority for the poetic juxtapositions and the meaningful analogical perceptions. In rejecting socially-approved values (both ancient and modern) to do with war, in social relations and the rejection of materialistic values, the authority for the truth of the analogy is not Propertius, but Pound. Yet Pound, as the author of such truth, only exists in the linguistic energies of the text, of the logopoeia which he brings to bear. The essential meaning of the work does not exist in the Propertian material at all, but rather in the associative ellipse between Propertius and the modern Pound.

From this arises the very peculiarly literary nature of logopoeia. Pound's writing had very often in practice been literary in its impulse. But logopeia *could not exist* without the pre-existing texts. It is only *against* the pre-existing that its *difference* can be determined.

This is the nature of the *Homage*. In the original *Elegies*, a kind of conscious distanciation is achieved in the ironic relationship between Propertius's self-mocking perception of the nature of Cynthia and the seriousness of the verse which derives from their relationship. On the level of diction, meaning is contained in such devices of *tone* as the disparity between hearty colloquialism and the formality of a high literary language. Pound may even have been drawn to Propertius's *Elegies* because he saw in the texts a problem of self-consistency and mimesis — that is between the reflection of reality and the mysterious intention of the poet — which had been one of his main interests since the writing of 'Near Perigord'.

In post-war London, it was the new American poet, T S Eliot, who seemed to Pound to combine logopoeic irony with phanopoeic directness:

'... his wholly unrealisable, always apt, half ironic suggestion, and his precise realisable picture. It would be possible to point out his method of conveying a whole situation and half a character by three words of a quoted phrase; his constant aliveness, his mingling of a very subtle observation with the unexpectedness of a backhanded cliché.'
(LE, 419)

It is wholly characteristic of Pound's methods that he does not proceed to do the pointing-out, but leaves the insight barely recorded. On the other hand, and equally characteristic, is the fact that the method Pound refers to here is fully realised in his *Homage to Sextus Propertius*. Besides himself and Eliot, Pound discovered one other writer in English whom he considered capable of logopoeia: James Joyce. In his Paris Letter to the *Dial* of May 1922 (an evaluation of *Ulysses*) Pound commented that 'Joyce satirises at least seventy varieties of style, and includes a whole history of English prose by implication', so that:

' . . . in the Cyclops episode we have a measuring of the difference between reality, and reality as represented in various lofty forms of expression; the satire on the various dead manners of language culminates in the execution scene, blood and sugar stewed into clichés and rhetoric. . . . ' (LE, 407)

Pound had originally perceived logopoeia as a division of poetic diction, but there is no effective reason for such a limitation in the case of a non-sensual, metalinguistic category, as the description of Joyce indicates. By the end of the London years, there was a sense in which Pound was perceiving logopoeia as a kind of evidence of intelligence. Remy de Gourmont provided the best example of this tendency. Pound's early interest in Gourmont was as a master of melopoeia;[10] but by the time of his major essay on Gourmont, Pound had come to see him as a kind of Voltairean polymath social critic in a battle with the intellectual and linguistic decadence of France. Gourmont's major influence on Pound's development has been described by several scholars.[11] Around 1918, Pound's writing was for a while full of direct and indirect references to Gourmont's intelligence in terms of a logopoeic intelligence:

' . . . an intelligence almost more than an artist . . . intensely aware of the differences of emotional timbre; and as a man's message is precisely his *façon de voir*, his modality of apperception, this particular awareness was his "message".' (LE, 340)

Pound's long essay on Gourmont avoids analysing his methods but again asserts very vigorously a series of 'facts' about his presentation of ideas to the end of social and artistic responsibility, in communications addressed to fellow-intellectuals of all nations. Pound affirms the efficacy of an individual intelligence in cultural reform. He himself adopted from Gourmont the phrase *'dissociation des idées'*. 'Dissociation of ideas' is the means of pursuing critical perceptions affecting the mental life of the society. Pound took it as the mark of a superior intelligence directed toward cultural analysis and criticism; for Gourmont it was the 'distinctions' of original analytical thought. To make
98

such dissociation of ideas is to destroy accepted associations and mental abstractions, or — specifically in terms of language — to abolish linguistic and hence mental clichés and outworn diction, by re-defining one's terms.

Gourmont wrote specifically on one concept which clearly had an important influence on Pound's thinking about logopoeia: the intellectual energy which enables elements of verbal clichés to be not only dissociated from the language, but re-associated in new patterns of relationship, so renewing the pereceptions which were their original source.[12] The clichés of the *Homage to Sextus Propertius*, signified by the stiffness of parodic language, relate the perceptions of Propertius to those of Pound, the new author. Both Propertius's own lost ironies, and the criticial awareness of Pound are illuminated by the re-associative process.

The logopoeic proposition of dissociation and renewal which Pound took from Gourmont led at the end of the London years to his critical-poetical strategy of using language for the re-shaping of meaning in the poetry. The purpose of the strategy is to tell truth, truth on both conceptual and verbal levels. Logopoeia is traditional, or historical, in its operation, in that it inevitably relates to a cultural theme. Many of Pound's essays from 1912 onwards related to a concern for the quality of the civilisation in which the poet lives and works; many of the poems deal overtly and comparatively with disjunctions between past and present. In T S Eliot's contemporary work, there is an overt awareness of cultural loss, an elegiac mood which became stronger as the years passed. In Pound's, the links between the present time and the remembered past are of a less simple nature, and nostalgia does not become the undercurrent of his work. Pound's allusive, logopoeic language does, however, insist upon using the terminology of historical specificity in places outside its usual stylistic context, creating a significant irony or attitude toward past and present. It also adopts material from the literatures of other cultures to comment on the local, contemporary idiom and social identity — which is the use of Propertius's *Elegies*, or the 'Nekuia' of Homer, used in Canto 1. Logopoeic adoptions operate on an associative, or metamorphic level, in that they call into being sudden luminous comparisons in the reader's mind. This illumination is an act of both criticism and education, and criticism and education are therefore the joint functions of much of the logopoeic poetry of the period.

Truth in the transitional poems
Between 1914 and 1920, Pound wrote four poems — perhaps they should be described as poem-sequences — which mark a transition from the comparatively simple, referential Imagist poetry to the more

99

complex, allusive and elliptical mode of the *Cantos*. These transitional sequences, which must be seen as developments of the linguistic and formal materials needed for the *Cantos*, were (in order of composition) 'Near Perigord', Cantos I to III published in *Poetry* in 1917 (the 'Ur-Cantos') but written and revised during the eight years 1915 to 1923, *Homage to Sextus Propertius* (1919), and *Hugh Selwyn Mauberley* (1920). All have been the objects of misunderstanding and debate. All present problems for most readers in terms of interpretation – the simplest decisions about meaning. Such problems need to be considered partly in terms of how Pound applied logopoeic verbal strategy in order to make a new kind of truth-statement about tradition, and the historical and cultural authority of the poem. The key lies in the relationship between the text of the poems and the world in which they were written, and to which they bear an uncertain mimetic relationship.

'Near Perigord' was largely written during 1913 and 1914. It has been neglected by many critics, either because it resembles many of the earlier poems using Provençal settings and the Browning manner, or perhaps because it is less obviously 'difficult' and *Cantos*-facing than the longer sequences which followed it. There is external evidence of its importance: in the 'Ur-Cantos', whose subject is the problem of writing, or setting out to write the projected modern epic, Pound was considering the possibility of taking Browning's 'Sordello' as his model, and using Bertran de Born as his own Sordello.[13] This at once provides a link between the theme of 'Near Perigord' and the 'Ur-Cantos' which followed it. Both can be seen as attempts to clear the ground for the great work which Pound proposed. Thematically, both share the riddle which is introduced also in Browning's poem of the availability of historical truth to the modern writer.

The apparent subject of 'Near Perigord' is the poem by Bertran de Born which Pound had adapted in 1908 as 'Na Audiart' (CSP, 22-3). Pound had returned to Bertran on several occasions subsequently, with his 'Planh for the young English king' (CSP, 50-1) and 'Sestina: Altaforte' (CSP, 42-3), as well as a variety of references in *The spirit of romance* and essays. Bertran also haunted a later poem, 'Provincia deserta', inspired by Pound's walking tour of Provence in 1912. Part of his interest was in the historical man: the epigraph to 'Sestina: Altaforte' is 'Eccovi! Judge ye! Have I dug him up again?' If the reader's answer to this is, Yes, it is Yes in terms of Browning's English style. This language makes the Bertran who is speaking the sestina a kind of late-Victorian gentleman-adventurer in mediaeval fancy dress; and the poem is a Browning-like dramatic monologue which presents and develops a personality, whose psychology explains and justifies what the text denotes. There is no real problem of interpretation in a persona poem of this kind, because the message of the poem,

100

and the character of the imaginary author, confirm one another. 'Provincia Deserta. (CSP, 131-3) and the slightly earlier translation of *'Dompna pois de me no'us cal'* (CSP, 115-7) are the next stage of the argument. 'Provincia deserta' works on a more subjective and meditative level than a *persona* poem:

> 'I have walked
>   into Perigord,
> I have seen the torch-flames, high-leaping . . . '   (CSP, 132)

Occasionally this first-person authorial voice changes into that of the old-fashioned Victorian tragedian, especially in passages of direct speech:

> 'I have said:
>   "Here such a one walked.
> Here Coeur-de-Leon was slain.
> Here was good singing. . . . " '   (CSP, 132-3)

Sometimes, however, this speaking voice faces into the images and snatches of conversation in the objective world he is offering us, for example in the passage beginning 'Two men tossing a coin . . . ' (CS, 133). The poem successfully states the poet's ability to achieve full understanding of the past through contact with its physical relics in the present: the emotional and intellectual reverberations produced by the possession of the objective, surviving historical artifact.

Probably 'Near Perigord' was begun close in time to the writing of 'Provincia deserta'; but it is a much more ambiguous and problematic work, and cost Pound considerable effort.[14] It negates the optimism and control of the other, and steps beyond both the simple persona-poem and the meditative, subjective lyric. The poem (CSP, 171-7) is a meditation on the relationship between the modern reader, a real poet with a historical existence in the past, and the poem, a text which has outlived both its author and its culture. 'Near Perigord' asks a series of questions about the nature and identity of a poet, the extent to which we can *know* the poet by reading a text which purports to express his meaning or intention. It questions the relationship between intention and text.

In structure, 'Near Perigord' (like the other transitional works) is a numbered sequence of poems without narrative development; the poems are differentiated from one another by tone. The first part, with its speaker, his question, and his auditor, reminds us of Pound's youthful taste for Browning. The riddle presented is that of a hidden significance: that is, how to determine the absolute truth, or how to find a single meaning or interpretation of a poem if one assumes that there is a truth which a man first of all 'knows' and then expresses in written discourse. Readers can perceive that there are various kinds of

101

alternative, mutually exclusive interpretations based on external evidence of the poet's intention — 'read between the lines of Uc St Circ' (CSP, 171) is an admonition which works like a scholarly footnote — or deduced logically from the geographical facts which Pound himself discovered during his walking trip. In 1913, with 'Provincia deserta', the obscurities of such work seemed to Pound to be capable of interpretation because he believed that they 'grew out of' the social conditions of the time and could therefore be unravelled by reference to social fact (LE, 94). But by the writing of 'Near Perigord', what is naively termed 'fact' in the poem is ambiguous, and remains so no matter how hard Pound stares at it. 'Is it a love poem? Did he sing of war?' Even Dante's authority is doubtful. The problem really lies in the disjunction between the poetic text and the man who was its author.

The second section suggests that a fiction can be created in the gap between extant historical text and the dead historical author, and that this fiction will explain them both. The poem moves close to the man's experience, to the historical Bertran (sharply seen as a poet resembling the descriptions of the young Pound, with a red beard and Ezra's 'green cat's eye'). The three movements of the section focus in turn on him, on Papiol's journey and its possible outcome, and on an imaginary conversation between Arnaut Daniel and Richard Plantagenet, in which *their* experience and interpretation of facts also remain ambiguous. The section culminates in a translation of six lines of Dante's fictional 'talk' (CSP, 176); at the end, interpretation once more fails. The final line — 'Or take En Bertrans?' — is the rhetorical signal that a different attempt will be made. It is this third attempt which makes a reader hesitate.

> 'Bewildering spring, and by the Auvezère
> Poppies and day's eyes in the green émail
> Rose over us. . . .'   (CSP, 176)

The first word announces a change in method: *bewildering* spring — the adjective is expressive, emotional, signifying change from meditated or reported to *felt* reality. Furthermore, the text shifts into the archaisms of late-Romantic diction. The effect of all this is to signal to the reader that he is now *inside* an experience. But who says these words? Whose reality is being expressed, whose head are we inside? It is interesting that even fairly recently some have read this section as Bertran's, some as Maent's. In the text published in 1915, two lines now deleted identify the words as Bertran's. Pound considered them redundant, and likely to weaken the section (Paige, 406). Who, then, is the author of this section?

That question cannot be answered by saying that there was, no doubt, an Ezra Pound who typed the words on paper, owned copyright,

102

arranged publication. But so in the same way did someone Pound knew as 'De Born', and even so Pound was left with the disjunction. I am using 'author' to mean, not the man with the typewriter (or the quill pen), but the authorial *function*, the source of the personal, historical or scientific authentication of truth.[15] In this sense, the reader sees a number of authors in the work. The first was the Browningesque monologuist who said, 'Solve me the riddle' and identified himself as the perceiver of an existing problem: he offered factual evidence, but he lacks the kind of implicit self-betrayal which serves to construct the rational personality of a narrative *character*, and hence the kind of authoritative validation of truth which we find in the speaker of a poem like 'My last duchess'. This monologuist makes no claim to be Ezra Pound, he is merely the perceiver of a riddle. In fact, by addressing 'Messire Cino' I think he can be said to imply his historical contemporaneity with Bertran, although his diction is Victorian English; but evidence of identity is so uncertain that it seems inappropriate to assign this author a name or being outside the text of the poem.

Next there is an 'author' in the second section who moves into fictional discourse and makes the claim to modernity in the phrase 'And we've the gossip (skipped six hundred years) . . . ' In what sense can *this* author claim the experience of watching Bertran, or witnessing a meeting between the poet, Arnaut Daniel, and the king, Richard? Arnaut, Richard and Dante are all, in turn, in some sense the authors of some phrases; but their relationship to a central authorial discourse is unclear, and the most significant link between the initial author and the author of the first section lies, I think, in their common tendency to use an impersonal version of the first-person plural 'we'/'us'.

But the power of the shift into the third section is underlined by the reader's recognition of the disjunction between this new 'we' and the previous ones: as it were, the real, experiencing 'we' against a previous editorial 'we'. By comparison, even in the penultimate section of 'Provincia deserta' (CSP, 133), where the bright images of the past seem absorbed into the author's experience, the first-person-singular narrator at least remained, as in one of Coleridge's conversation poems, holding the text in one single movement out and back again, from beginning to end. We know *there* whose ground we stand on.

In 'Near Perigord' there is no such ultimate author, no such movement in the single consciousness between past and present, memory and experience — rather a series of egos: three, four (counting 'Dante writes', although of course his lines, despite their rhetorical power and climactic positioning, have no greater claim to transcendentally-truthful interpretation than any other), and more. All make a series of attempts, theories, subjective views.

There remains the problem of what seems to be presented as

103

the ultimate statement of a transcendent truth in the final strong lines:

> 'She who could never live save through one person,
> She who could never speak save to one person,
> And all the rest of her a shifting change,
> A broken bundle of mirrors . . . !'   (CSP, 177)

The poem breaks off. These are not the lines of the 'Bertran-author' of the rest of this section. They comment critically on his discourse and its relation to the historical woman who was its point of reference to reality. The lines are important: by their verbal parallels, their strong metres and their position in the poem, they offer us the 'answer' to the initial riddle: they claim to be the truth. What they say is that Maent is/ was a certain kind of being, unable to shape her world but reflecting aspects of it – a kind of thirteenth century Mauberley, as we shall see. In addition, the lines suggest something quite complex about the way in which such a flux is caught in the Image of poetry: that Maent exists neither independently, nor in a poet's intention, but as a surface grasped only in the organisation of an utterance: a signification. They say that Maent is the subject of the language of the poem and has no existence as a closed event. The 'broken bundle of mirrors' is *both* reflective (referential) *and* fragmented, unknowable.

What validates this statement? What makes it true? Or to put it another way, on what basis do we accept the validity of these four lines? How can a reader evaluate their truth even in the limited sense of being certain that they apply to the riddle posed, much less assess whether they fulfil their rhetorical promise of being a transcendent truth? For if we cannot identify a *single* authorial voice (whether belonging to a character, a historical personage, or an omniscient narrator) leading us through the whole text from beginning to end, and if instead we have a series of authors, different authors for different truths, then we have abandoned authorial expression as a principle of textual unity and textual interpretation or closure, and need to find some other way of comprehending the irresolvable contradictions within the poem. And if the search for this unity fails, then we have of course the alternative of saying that this is the kind of poem which many readers have seen in the *Cantos*: an anthology of structureless fragments, touched by image and lyric beauty, but incapable of any interpretation in logical terms (that is, in terms of cause and effect), so entirely accidental and therefore effectively *meaningless*: scarcely even the kind of statement that can be 'untrue'.

The failure of the search for a narrative structure in the *Cantos* has on occasion led readers to condemn it as a hotch-potch of references for tracing, foreign phrases for translating, historical names for identify-

104

ing: a game for the crossword puzzle enthusiast to solve by means of some immense ideal *Index to the cantos*. What I have been arguing is that the nature of the ideal index is the nature of the text without an Author. In the 'Ur-Cantos' Pound was looking for the author for his poem: the man with an intentional blue-print precedent to the poem as written, to which the text, as a fixed product of his expression, could be compared. There is no such author in 'Near Perigord' (although there are authors), and 'Near Perigord' records Pound's rejection of this kind of authorial function, giving the reason for the rejection: he has discovered that it fails. Instead, Pound was making a faltering discovery of a new kind of objective voice. 'Near Perigord' is a warning to the readers of the other poems, who face a *Homage to Sextus Propertius* whose author is never only Propertius, but never quite Ezra Pound; a *Mauberley* where critics have argued endlessly about where 'EP' ends and 'Mauberley' begins his story and what is the status and value of the poems 'Envoi' and 'Medallion'; and finally the *Cantos*, where Pound first sought an author and then rejected him, 'Ur-Cantos' and all: 'But Sordello? And my Sordello?' The early *persona* poems have always been thought of as poems in which Pound hid himself behind the mask of another whose emotions and understanding these poems expressed. They have been discussed as a kind of dramatising strategy. But they are simple poems to interpret because the ego of a personal mask is always there. The poems are devised as expressive works, explorations of someone's experience. What was happening between 1913 and 1915 — between Imagism and Vorticism — was that 'Ezra Pound' was beginning to efface himself, not by putting on a mask and pretending to express someone else's experience, but by moving away altogether from the fictional representation of a personal truth, away from the representation of external reality, away from linear structure of discourse into a more complex presentational and relational mode of objective truthfulness. 'Near Perigord' is the first, and in this way the most transitional, of the poems in which this is occurring, it is the earliest long poem which faces squarely the problems raised by Pound's first, Romantic, expressive notions of poetry. Even as late as 1913, when he wrote his important essay on 'The serious artist' (LE, 41-57) Pound still more or less assumed that a poem *expresses* an emotional, subjective truth; but he was also asserting that the propriety of creative literature lies in the *precision* with which that expression is formulated. That is precisely where 'Provincia deserta' stands, and 'Near Perigord' begins. Hence the initial riddle about the meaning of 'Dompna pois . . .': whether it is the expression of a subjective truth transcending the social truth of fictional narrative, or whether it is somehow insincere and therefore, according to 'The serious artist', immoral or meaningless (LE, 44). In the Imagist/Vorticist series of

105

essays called 'Affirmations', which he published in *The new age* in January and February, 1915, Pound showed his concern for finding a means of making truth entirely objective; in a review of 1918, he applauds Wyndham Lewis's proposition that a 'condition of art' is to 'have no inside' (LE, 430) or subjective motivation. The total objectification of authorial perceptions is embodied in cumulative references to concrete particulars. This removes and distances the potentially-limited, potentially-biassed author from the poem, which I suspect is the point of the third section of 'Near Perigord'. The authentication of a poetic statement cannot depend on the poet's personal authority. Indeed the author's existence is deduced only from the objective fact of a pattern of words or names, signs arranged in a manner analogous to the arrangements of planes or colours in the visual arts: meaning arises from relationships. Words themselves denote *real* things; but their relationship does not simply express the poet's meaning. Even the very linearity of syntax becomes doubtful, as an expression of meaning: we depend instead on the apparent paradox of unrepeated pattern-units, of broken bundles of mirrors, of what Pound in 'Affirmations' called a 'musical conception of form' consisting of elements which can be shuffled into new, meaningful formal combinations.[16]

If 'Near Perigord' can be seen as a kind of working out of Vorticist aesthetic theory, then the third section must be seen in terms of the psychological event of the Image. This event is presented as Maent's *only* reality, for only those words can speak to the reader, and neither Maent herself, nor any 'author' standing behind or above who could tell the truth in some other words. There is *no* mimetic representation of Maent, apart from that Image. From this point in Pound's poetry, it becomes clear that there is no other way of perceiving truth in art: the poem is a discourse whose words constantly and repeatedly disappoint any readerly expectation of a consistent authorial being and therefore of either an intention distinct from its textual realisation (for the various explanations which Pound gave of the nature of *Propertius*, the structure of the *Cantos*, or whatever, came not only after the event but in response to the disappointment of those expectations I have mentioned) or any hierarchy of discourses. Sometimes — the American history cantos are one example — Pound's text makes an objective use of reality by quoting historical documents at some length, so that we almost forget the kind of authorial expectations which are based on familiar literary conventions. We *appear* to be reading history rather than a literary discourse; although of course even here we do not have unmediated reality — the selections have been chosen from widely different sections of a source-book — and it is merely a kind of provisional strategy of history which is always present as a gesture to replace authority of literary discourses. Again, the reader's literary (authorial)

106

expectations may be re-aroused by the reappearance in the text of some kind of biographical detail in association with other kinds of experience and a different style and tone: as in the subjective lyric of the *Pisan cantos*.[17] Therefore, despite such gestures of historical authenticity, the text cannot present itself as a sequence of words moving toward a pre-existant truth. From the moment of 'Near Perigord', the *Cantos* would remain an overtly open text, a 'draft'. All intentional pattern — the intention of a closure within one hundred cantos, for example, or the intention of a closure by means of fulfilling a fugal structure, or of a closure by means of the tripartite metaphysical structure of a divine comedy — all these require an author. They require the coincidence of expression with intention, poem with man. Pound abandoned such patterns when he found that they could only present an incomplete and ambiguous truth.

He may never have conceptualised the inescapable conclusion to which 'Near Perigord' had brought him; later theorists of literature have done so in describing literary discourse as:

' . . . a multidimensional space in which a variety of writings, none of them original, blend and clash. The text is a tissue of quotations drawn from the innumerable centres of culture. . . . The writer can only imitate a gesture that is always anterior, never original.'[18]

This is the unspoken summary of Pound's traditionalism, his theory of poetry as language, and the practice of his post-Vorticist poetry.

After Perigord
The mystery of the relationship between the poetic text and the real world was a problem to which Pound returned on several occasions. The 'Ur-Cantos' of 1915-1917 debate the role of the poet and his artifact in a voice which is the direct, confessional statement of the poet. Traces of the debate remain in the published version:

> 'Hang it all, Robert Browning,
> There can be but the one "Sordello."
> But Sordello, and my Sordello?
> *Lo Sordels si fo di Mantovana.*'   (Cantos, 2/6)

The fourth line quotes the opening of a *razo*, or critical life of the historical Sordello who lived, wrote poems, and made apparent 'truth-statements' which survived him. The reference to Browning and the title 'Sordello' suggest that to Pound the historical person survived rather in Browning's poem of 1840 — a poem which in the 'Ur-Cantos' year of 1915 Pound described as 'certainly the best long poem in English since Chaucer' (Paige, 406), and whose opening lines are themselves a meditation on whether a modern poet can 'make-new' the past: a theme which is extensively repeated in both 'Near Perigord' and the 'Ur-Cantos' themselves. Both the quoted reference and this allusion therefore refer to the kind of historically ambiguous reality which is represented in the surviving texts of Bertan de Born, Propertius's *Elegies* (or Pound's *Cantos*).

'Ur-Canto' I begins, like 'Provincia deserta', by superimposing an authorial Pound on his literary-historical forebears and on the unfinished texts which give him their experience — texts which Pound has already recognised to be ambivalent reflections of truth. Versions of the three 'Ur-Cantos'[20] retain a reasonably consistent authorial strategy by using conversational modern colloquialisms and rhetorical 'asides'. Arising from this approach, however, is the problem of the incompleteness of subjective truth: the 'Ur-Cantos' ask *which author* is capable of telling absolute truth. Pound proposes a series of *personae*: Browning/Sordello, Chaucer, Arnaut, Catullus, Propertius, Li Po — and places his project beside their texts, superimposing theirs upon his own potential text and his past work on theirs. The future text, extant texts and others' original texts are held together in a meditation on the intertextuality of the poetic project and the unknowability of a real world which is of the past, fragmented in ambivalent documents and held in the memory. 'Ur-Canto' I proposes to assume Browning's mode of discourse, which Pound saw as a meditative narrative, half dramatic and half epic,[21] and use it as he had already done in 'Near Perigord' as an inclusive, objective mode of discourse to state the truth about the world.

The 'Ur-Cantos' were Pound's false start, revised out of recognition in the early sections of the final version, where his strategy had resolved itself into an ideogrammic discourse. But the questions of the first attempt had by no means been settled within it. *Propertius* also approaches the mystery of the existence of an historical poem and the extent to which any statement which it makes remains comprehensible. The problematic of the *Homage to Sextus Propertius* is close to that of 'Near Perigord: to what extent can the reader say that Propertius 'loved' Cynthia: was it a love poem, or did he really prefer to sing of war? Here, as also in the beginning of the second part of 'Near Perigord', the nature of authorial validation comes into question. The title warns us that the 'author' of what we read is not, *cannot* be, the Roman poet: he is the object of the 'homage', not the subject of the poem.[22] But the text equally implies that the author is not Ezra, for it refers directly to experience which is not of the twentieth century, especially to mythological elements lost to the modern audience. The kind of truth which this poem tells is centred in the gap between the two poets and their artistic beliefs, and is the link between them, as we have already seen. Insofar as this relationship is expressed by the words of the text, they are the only means of expressing and validating the authority of the 'homage' and the things which it asserts to be true.

To what extent Pound was aware of the theoretical implications of this work remains uncertain. He defended his 'translation' by referring to Propertius's intentions (Letters, 246) as though rejecting the lesson of 'Near Perigord'. He also described the sequence as though it were an old-fashioned *persona*-poem.[23] He tended in fact to appeal to the author and his intentions, even as his linguistic strategy removed the very authority to which he could appeal.

Finally there was *Hugh Selwyn Mauberley*, considered by many readers to be the best of Pound's verse. Published at the end of his years in London, and seen by Pound himself as the ultimate statement about the culture in which he lived, and in which the Vorticist Renaissance had failed,[24] this is the most complete, most 'difficult' of the logopoeic works. The meaning of this poem-sequence is largely contained in its tone, and this in turn depends on a complex of verbal and literary associations, manipulated in the text by its devices of quotation, distortion, historical reference, and apparently-objective critical comment. The sequence manipulates literary tradition once again; and in this manipulation much of the significance resides. The poem both states and illustrates the dichotomy between a set of eternal, recurring cultural values, and the devaluation of such things in twentieth-century London. Thus it foreshadows the *Cantos*.

Mauberley begins by establishing a personal author; this is done by means of apparently-personal references: the initials 'EP' head the first poem (CSP, 205) which also mentions a 'half-savage' birth-place and the thirty-first year of age.[25] The reader will readily identify these as references to Ezra Pound's life, although their significance does not reside in historical accuracy so much as their gesture toward it. Their presence suggests that we are embarking upon a confessional poem and warns us to expect to identify the truth of its references by appealing to historical (real, autobiographical) events. The work begins, in other words, by claiming to be a mimetic statement reflecting real life and Pound's experience of it.

To follow this direction in order to interpret *Mauberley* is to look for answers to a number of questions which the text proposes. Among the simpler questions are the identification of a number of proper names either historical — foetid Buchanan, Lionel Johnson, Burne-Jones — or pseudonymous — Brennbaum, Mr Nixon, 'the stylist' (the presence of recognisable proper names always leads a reader to assume that the unrecognisable ones can be historically identified, given some kind of external knowledge, a key to meaning). The major critical question which has been asked repeatedly, frequently answered and never quite settled can be summarised as this one: What is the identity of the 'I' explicit or implicit in the poem; or, from whose point of view are judgements constantly being made? For example, what is the relationship between 'EP', whose tomb is designated in the first poem, and the name Ezra Pound' on the title page; and what is the relationship between either or both of them and the H S Mauberley whose name stands at the beginning of the second sequence of poems with the date 1920 (CSP, 216)?

The problem seems to be that the reader is just as uncertain about Pound's intentions in writing *Hugh Selwyn Mauberley* as Pound had been of Bertran de Born's — or more; for 'Near Perigord' at least accepts the existence of only two clear, if mutually exclusive, interpretations of 'Dompna pois'. As with both 'Near Perigord' and *Propertius*, Mauberley sets the general and traditional (the classical) against the personal and immediate. The situation in which the three poets — EP, Mauberley and Pound — live is seen against a tradition compounded of literary, historical and social elements which are alluded to by means of the use of proper names with their associations, passages of Latinised diction so formal that they seem to mock what they purport to express, quotations which at once carry with them a textual fact and (particularly when deliberate misquotation occurs) point up its peculiar relevance to the contemporary situation, and clichés signifying thought-habits which both carry the overt message of the poem, and hold that content with its habitual contexts up to ridicule. The dominant tone is therefore ironical, and that irony is controlled by the ambiguity of such devices. John J Espey's study of *Mauberley* describes these linguistic usages in some detail and demonstrates the uses Pound made of a literary tradition derived from Gautier, Henry James and Remy de Gourmont.[26] It is useful work; though an equally useful gloss of the sequence will be found in Pound's own 1918-1919 essays on James and Gourmont (LE, 259-338, 339-58). Pound himself described *Mauberley* as both a 'study in form' and an attempt to condense a James novel (Letters, 248). The poem also contains condensed allusions, of all the types listed, to Homer, Sappho, Ovid, the Pre-Raphaelites, Coleridge, Ruskin, Swinburne, the poets of the Rhymers Club, Johnson, Waller, Lawes, Flaubert, Jacquemart, Pier Francesca, Pisanello and others, many rhetorically associated with the making of some kind of value-judgement.

The two poems 'Medallion' (CSP, 222) and 'Envoi (1919)' (CSP, 215) are both in themselves quotations; they appear, if only from their climactic positions, to imply some formal closure to each section which, in turn, suggests a value-judgement whose exact nature is by no means clear.

A meaning which depends on tonal evaluation-by-association inevitably leaves readers uncertain of their interpretation of a given passage, as well as the whole related sequence of passages. For example: at the beginning of poem XII (CSP, 213-4) there is one juxtaposition which makes a fairly simple, though implicit, comparison of traditional values. Our interpretation of the passage is assisted not only by the comparatively conventional nature of the contrast with which much post-Romantic literature has probably left readers fairly familiar, but because the clarity seems to be assisted by the addition of objective comment:

> ' "Daphne with her thighs in bark
> Stretches toward me her leafy hands," –
> Subjectively. In the stuffed-satin drawing-room
> I await The Lady Valentine's commands,
>
> Knowing my coat has never been
> Of precisely the fashion
> To stimulate, in her,
> A durable passion; . . . '

Associations of the nature-myth with its echoes of transcendent love are juxtaposed with the social connotations of stuffed-satin parlours and the 'fashion' which, with the word positioned at the end of a run-on line, carries with it associations of fashion *tout court*, the interests of an artificial society, as well as the 'fashion to stimulate', associated in its rhyme-echo with 'passion', both devaluing and being devalued by it. Other things could be said about the contrast of the self-immolating passion and self-aggrandising vanity, about the temporal analogy between the outmoded coat and the durability of passion, about the stammer of the shortened lines of the second stanza, and the hiccup of the phrase 'in her' with its surrounding, hesitant commas. The point is that a dichotomy is being set up between nature and natural passion, and the artifices and oppressiveness of contemporary society – a dichotomy not expressed in the interpretative comment of a narrative voice, but derived from the associations of the contextualised images, the jog-trot doggerel of the second stanza, the drawl of long vowels, the subjective attitude implied by the clichés 'other strata', 'a possible friend and comforter', and the self-mocking 'which the highest cultures have nourished', or 'long-since superseded'. There may be other levels of meaning to be gained by the reader experienced enough to identify an echo of T S Eliot's 'Prufrock', the Laforguian stanza form and reference to Gautier's *Emaux et camées*, and the quotation from Pound's own early poem, 'The tree' (CSP, 17), setting up ironic echoes with the social context of its would-be-smart young author and alerting the reader instantly, by placing the present work in the specific context of Pound's whole poetry, of the intertextuality of his writing, of the meaning in the elliptical relationship between this poem and that. But what if these, or some part of them, are not available to the reader?

This of course is the real problem of interpretation with *Mauberley*, as with the *Cantos* to come, and indeed to a greater or lesser extent all

111

allusive, post-Baudelairean modernist poetry based on associative methods and apparently requiring some kind of interpretation of the elements of significance in a method which is essentially connotative. Worse, there are other sections of *Mauberley* where logopoeic juxtaposition is as prominent as in poem XII, but its significations are more obscure because the meaning is not so clearly supported by its metrical and denotative devices. In 'Yeux glauques', for example, meaning is communicated (if at all) in ellipses between juxtaposed objects:

> 'Gladstone was still respected,
> When John Ruskin produced
> "Kings' Treasuries"; Swinburne
> And Rossetti still abused.
>
> Foetid Buchanan lifted up his voice
> When that faun's head of hers
> Became a pastime for
> Painters and adulterers.
>
> The Burne-Jones cartons
> Have preserved her eyes;
> Still, at the Tate, they teach
> Cophetua to rhapsodise;
>
> Thin like brook-water,
> With a vacant gaze.
> The English Rubaiyat was still-born
> In those days.'

(CSP, 209)

Patterns of repetition, either of phrases ('still respected'/'still abused') or materials ('become a pastime'/'have preserved'), involving time-shifts, make it evident that a process of comparison links aesthetic, moral and social values. On the other hand, syntactical links and the causal relations which these signify are almost entirely absent. It seems impossible to identify very clearly any consistent poetic tone in this passage;[27] tone, as an indicator of authorial stance, depends on the logopoeic cluster of words and associations representing attitudes. The signs within these clusters are mostly proper names and historical allusions, and apparently they require the reader to share the poet's familiarity with details of the Pre-Raphaelite movement. The title of the poem is no key to the work; it is obscurely associative, suggesting to the knowledgeable reader the myth of Glaucus, or some kind of sea-change into immortality. If the poem in fact maintained a clear mimetic relationship with cultural history and its artifacts, then its interpretation could be accomplished by referring to external records: meaning could thus be identified rather than elicited, and wholly open to the reader with the correct education. An identification of all the allusions is

112

theoretically possible, and some such attempt is the most common way of dealing with an obscurely allusive poetry. Peter Brooker, in his *Student's guide to the selected poems of Ezra Pound*[28] offers a sound recent example of this kind of gloss, for he not only identifies allusions historically, but traces their other appearances in Pound's writings (always one of the most useful interpretative methods in Pound's case, for his writing is highly repetitive and accretional). There are no objections to Brooker's identifications. However, the most informative aspect of his material is not the identifications themselves, but the extensions of them to trace a context of usage peculiar to Pound: an insight into the associations which these names and terms possessed for him, which allows us to deduce by external evidence the nature of Pound's critical judgements of the Aesthetic tradition in nineteenth century England. In other words, the scholar is providing the 'author' whom the poem lacks.

Textual analysis of course provides some other clues, as for instance when 'foetid' supplies an authorial attitude to the critic Buchanan but does so without historical specificity: the reader is given an attitude without understanding its factual basis in real life. We are left with a text which is making a gesture toward the real, while understanding is left to the reader's individual, pre-existing knowledge *unless it can somehow be inferred from the total poetic context.* Now, that context is one of aesthetic evaluation based on moral rather than critical grounds: the poem's theme; but there is a gap between the general context and the specific instance. Such an ellipse may sometimes contribute to the meaning of the poem, for the 'pastness' of some part of the cultural tradition may actually be signified by the very obscurity of reference. It is a signal to the partial memory, and a strand of the meaning is in a reference to the remoteness of traditional values, both moral and cultural, from the contemporary socio-historical context which had been established in the five war poems immediately preceding 'Yeux glauques' (CSP, 205-8). Therefore 'Yeux glauques' is a transitional poem, between the loss of cultural values in general, and the specific losses exemplified in Mr Nixon's hack-writer's advice, the physical withdrawal of 'the stylist', and the artificial social complex of the 'conservatrix of Milesian' suburban pretender, and the Lady Valentine of high society.

What remains very much less clear is the question of any causal relationship between the first five poems and the remaining seven in the first sequence, and between 'Envoi (1919)' and the rest. The conventional syntax, traditional literary diction and metrical form, and the contrasting cultural materials of the last poem mark it as belonging to a different world of discourse. Actually, the reader of *Mauberley* is faced simultaneously with a range of problems: the need to identify the historical references (that is, provided we are so rash as to assume the

113

reality of the mimetic gestures which the sequence makes), the need to come to a correct understanding of the associations which are trailed like a bullfighter's cape by a variety of allusions in the text, and the need to come to a correct contextual judgement of the ellipses within the poem caused by juxtaposition of elements of discourse in a strategy of communication. If we assume that the sequence possesses a mimetic basis — if, as several references might lead us to think, the poem makes *autobiographical* references to the poet, Pound — then we will need to interpret the sequence in terms of an authorial attitude toward, for example, the differences between the twentieth century and the nineteenth in literary London, as between the modern world and the ancient. Yet the poem itself clearly warns us against desiring the mimetic (CSP, 206).

There are movements within the sequence — for example, the first, savage poems on war — where an implicit authorial attitude coincides consistently with the stated truth in a logopoeic discourse of clichés (marked by inverted commas), significant allusions such as the quotation from Villon in poem I (CSP, 205) which is an elegy on the vanishing of the poet-hero, and cultural metaphors of an open and public nature:

> 'Faun's flesh is not to us,
> Nor the saint's vision.
> We have the press for wafer;
> Franchise for circumcision.'   (CSP, 207)

But for long passages, no such consistent and open viewpoint exists, hence the arguments among Pound scholars about the precise point at which Ezra Pound buries the 'EP' of the poem like an outworn mask — whether inside poem I, 'Ode pour l'election de son sepulchre', or at the end of the first part with the appropriately-named valedictory of 'Envoi' (a judgement which would in its turn affect how we evaluate 'Envoi' itself, for scholars are in equal disagreement about whether it is a merely derivative love lyric illustrating the decay of the English Renaissance, or an image of the 'sublime in the old sense' (CSP, 205) which brings into the text an example of the lost beauty of immortal art to compare with the meretricious and prostituted beauty of the day, or something else still). What Pound *intended*, by completing the two sections with 'Envoi (1919)' and 'Medallion' remains uncertain. There can be an agreement, based on the fact that each one ends a movement of the whole, that they somehow represent two paradigms and are therefore in one sense the subject of the work.[29] Interpretation of *Mauberley* as a whole must in this case depend on our precise understanding of the significance of the two poems, or the terms of their allusions, their role in literary tradition, their position in the structure of the sequence.

What does a poem like *Mauberley* represent? Must we read it by assuming that it is an essentially representational (mimetic) work which mirrors selected aspects of Pound's social and intellectual world, and depends on the identification of the elements which are represented? But the statement that 'the "age demanded" chiefly a mould in plaster' (CSP, 206) is made in a context which obviously rejects demands for an authenticity which is loosely representational, rather than either the unbending classical text, or the energetic, creative Vorticist poem.

Or is the real problem one of a logopoeic development of ironical discourse, effecting a distancing of the reader from the world of the poem and its values, in which understanding is not based on the identification of the terms in a representational equation, but rather on determining the precise degree of self-awareness, in order to understand the relationship in any passage between the point of view it presents and any identifiable consistent viewpoint as of, for instance, an author? If the tone of the text is too inherently ambivalent for the purpose, then the reader may look for external evidence in order to establish some consistency of import. But it is dangerous, obviously, to speculate or even to 'know' about the autobiographical or historical materials which went into the text if such knowledge makes us want to argue the connotative and associative significance of textual elements.

The arguments about the conceptual affect of the proper names used in the first poem of the second, 'Mauberley 1920', section is an example of this. It is possible to argue about the import of almost any detail:

' "His true Penelope
Was Flaubert,"
And his tool
The engraver's.' (CSP, 216)

Inverted commas mark a quotation from the first sequence and should remind of the self-imposed standards of 'EP'; but the discourse does not tell us authoritatively whose perception this memory is — whether the author of the statement is applying it in memory to EP seen in contrast to Mauberley as a rebel and hero, or whether in this context the author approves or disapproves of the prose, Flaubertian *mot juste* and verbal engraver's tool, much less whether in the social context this sort of engraving is all that can be expected.

The second poem in the 'Mauberley' section provides similar but even more extensive problems of interpretation as it drifts into an anonymous stream-of-consciousness whose author or validating authority remains stubbornly 'absent'. Earlier versions of this poem[30] give a rather clearer verbal clue to the import, as for example when a deleted version of the sixth stanza tries out a series of variants, including

115

'project' and 'delineate' for 'convey the relation', (CSP, 217). The synonyms pile up, communicating hesitant obsession with minute detail. In an excised stanza nine, the same device emphasised the passing of time and described Mauberley's 'non-perception' as a measure of his deadly anaesthesis. As Pound worked toward the published text, he deleted this kind of descriptive, omniscient comment which limits interpretation, and he left the text stronger but also more open, its meaning dependent on associations, heavy ellipses, and the insertion instead of inverted commas to imply a verbal cliché, throwing its own doubt on the validity of the purported statement.

There is of course an alternative authorial strategy for this poem. It echoes several elements of Pound's vorticist aesthetic: the true poem, like a vortex, is a pattern-creating energy working through the direct diction of the prose tradition in verse. Mauberley's 'invitation to perceptivity' can be seen as leading him toward an excessive concern for recording detail, or impressionism:

'The followers of Flaubert deal in exact presentation. The are often so intent on exact presentation that they neglect intensity, selection, and concentration. They are perhaps the most clarifying and they have been perhaps the most beneficial force in modern writing.' (LE, 399-400)

The psychology of the Mauberley figure lacks energy, or *virtù*, the selective, order-making energy; and any statement of which he is the author must be understood in this light. The single impression is Mauberley's de-energised unit of expression, held in no magnetic field and forming no whole (PD, 119-20). Mauberley himself rejects the extensive mimesis of realism only to be caught in the detail of his subject-matter: he reacts to the physical world by reflecting it rather than asserting the shaping power of the true artist's full, whole gaze. In an argument of this kind, the authorial validation is supplied not by a viewpoint within the poem — this is too ambiguous, too inconsistent — but by a conceptual background supplied from other texts. In the final poems of the sequence, the diction itself is illuminated by an essay published in 1915 in which Pound had discussed 'types' of poets in terms *Mauberley* echoes:

'These are bad expressions if they lead you to think of the artists as wholly passive, as a mere receiver of impressions. The good artist is perhaps a good seismograph, but the difference between man and a machine is that man . . . can, within limits, not only record but create.' (S Pr, 346)[31]

Thus the ellipses and associations of *Hugh Selwyn Mauberley* can largely be interpreted intertextually — traced into the critical essays of the few years preceding its composition. This would imply that Pound's aim was less to condense a novel, than delineate alternating authorial
116

identities in a social and aesthetic relationship. Those authors — 'EP' and Mauberley — are juxtaposed just as Propertius and Pound were in the earlier poem, and with as unclear a boundary between them. They are presented as, on the one hand, 'EP' directing the energy of his passion and intelligence against the *linguistic* circumstances represented in the war poems (although what 'Envoi 1919' seems to tell us is that his own linguistic powers were too traditionalistic entirely to fulfil their task) and on the other hand as the reactive Mauberley, who merely reflects his world minutely.[32] Setting 'Medallion' in the context of 'Envoi' is to juxtapose a diction with a diction, phanopoeia and melopoeia, Laforgue against Waller, and finally the intractable portrait of a twentieth-century Maent, whose form has been wrested from the sea of contemporary flux where Mauberley floats not entirely unproductively, if passively,[33] against the clear, conventional Renaissance challenge to mortality based on the creation of the singer and the art of the love poem. The truth of these two poems is not conceptually-based; it is in the alternative authorial strategies of the two texts and their relationship.

It would be possible to argue that the truth-statement of the whole sequence is most easily interpreted by context — by turning to the texts of Pound's prose, and seeing his vocabulary as word-counters, or signposts to interpretation, in a code system which straddles both poems and essays. In this procedure we would be recreating an absent validating author from the descriptive and discursive prose discourse, inserting it into the ellipses of the poetic text. This is to assume that *Hugh Selwyn Mauberley* is making the same type of statement which the criticisms make: that it is itself both theory and practice, or both criticism and the product of criticism: selection and presentation of the elements of a tradition, and an implicit statement about their use in a specific social context. *Mauberley*'s truth is embodied in a constantly-fluctuating set of associations and juxtapositions. The connective of overriding authorial statement has been removed, leaving the skeletal form of images to associate the creative passion of the discriminating, 'serious' artist in a variety of modes appropriate to many historical ages, with the absence of such passion and the impressionism of a diluter, a minor poet. The argument of the poem is analogous rather than causal. Its analogies are expressed by means of the logopoeic manipulation of diction and the juxtaposition of non-descriptive details. The whole is a unified, if elliptical, statement in both style of discourse and concepts, about the nature of a society and the permanent essence and function of art.

The ideogram of knowledge
The discovery which Pound had made during the writing of the transitional poems was, in a way, the discovery of *absence*: the absence of

117

ellipses in discourse and the validating author, the openness of a text whose meaning is not limited to the text of the poem but arises out of it from the energies of phanopoeia and extends beyond the words on the page to their relationships. The whole drift of Pound's theory had been toward an emphasis on writing as a system of relationships depending on arrangements of language. The most vital interest of *The spirit of romance* was in metaphor; the 'swift perception of relations' arising out of metaphor and similar linguistic usages (SR, 158) was the element of poetic communication which roused Pound to his vivid comparison of Shakespeare and Dante. The 'Osiris' essays formulate a concept of 'luminous details' and their relationships. Pound's development from a simple view of symmetrical form to a concept of absolute form, fluid form, allowed for a form of the whole work including both the text and its absences. Finally, his rejection of abstract discursive logic in favour of a unified statement based on the juxtaposition of elements and a lightning stroke of understanding – Imagism's complex – led on toward the Vorticist emphasis on formal energy, energy holding all the elements of the work in a unity.

During his struggle to reform the diction of poetry, Pound's reading of French literature led him to conceive of a 'prose tradition' in verse, which described for him a kind of literary language which permitted the clear and objective presentation of truth in poetry. He wrote of a poetic practice consisting of:

'... constatation of facts. It presents. It does not comment. It is irrefutable because it does not present a personal prediliction for any particular fraction of the truth. .... It is not a criticism of life, I mean it does not deal in opinion.'[34]

A statement of this kind is supported by his insistence, in other essays of the time, like 'The serious artist', of the role of poetry as objective, scientific truth-statements (LE, 50). Pound was attempting to define a method of making truth-statements in poetry which would wholly avoid the subjective, the opinionated, the accidental. A 'constation' of facts is a cluster of words (names) directly denoting elements of the real world. The word, from the French *constater*, defines a process of *establishing certain truth*. Natural or objective or 'presented' truth is associated linguistically with the use of the Flaubertian *mot juste*.[35] Functionally, it is associated with the search for a means of recording humanity and human life 'scientifically'; but in claiming that a literature which works by the constatation of facts actually possesses the quality of 'Nature',[36] Pound was saying that its status is the same as that of unmediated reality. Poetry composed by such a method is therefore *not* mimetic, does not mirror reality but is, ontologically, Reality itself.

118

In making such claims for the objective truthfulness of literary practice, Pound was being led into a formal, organisational principle which would be elastic enough to encompass reality in an open text, and at the same time would enable the poet successfully to communicate his broad, precise meaning to his reader. A poem with the status of reality, whose method and meaning both depend to a large extent on the relationship of elements, is potentially extensive. Pound developed a concept of mind as thought-processes responding to a meaningful conjunction of factual elements. There is a parenthetical paragraph in one of his sociocultural essays of 1919 in which he writes of a method (not unlike the method of luminous detail) of quoting touchstone-like 'snippets' in order to 'build up a concept of wrong, or right, of history':

'I put down these pellets in this manner not merely as a confession of how I catch myself thinking, but because other people think no better, because the burnt-in detail is tied by no more visible cords to the next detail. . . . '[37]

A few years later, he had expanded this subjective perception into the assertion of principle that 'All knowledge is built up from a rain of factual atoms. . . ' (GK, 98). What remains, of course, is the psychological basis with its linguistic consequences. Not only is symmetrical form abandoned here: so is the logic of ordinary syntax, for 'We no longer think or need to think in terms of a monolinear logic, the sentence structure, subject, predicate, object, etc' but instead are capable of 'thoughts that join like spokes in a wheel-hub that fuse in hyper-geometric amalgams'.[38]

Of course it can be argued[39] that Pound's attitude to diction had always been asyntactical: that his poetry reveals a special sensitivity to the texture of language, to rhythms, to individual words repeated in almost talismanic patterns. Furthermore, the constatation bears a close resemblance to the Image as emotional and intellectual complex, with its recognitions based on contiguities rather than mere resemblances. This much was established in his work before he received Ernest Fenellosa's papers and discovered in *The Chinese written character as a medium for poetry* a description of the Chinese ideogram as a direct, natural, asyntactical written mode which was capable of communicating simply and objectively with observant common sense (ABC, 21-3). What is significant for his later theory and, above all, poetic practice is the way in which asyntactical linguistic usage is supported by a certain theory of knowledge and its transmission. What Pound called the 'ideogram' is not a picture. It is the form which the process of perception takes, and the means of acquiring and transmitting knowledge (LE, 61).

The so-called 'ideogrammic method', which Pound both discussed

119

and demonstrated in his last book of criticism, his *Guide to Kulchur* (1938), consists of 'presenting one facet and then another until at some point one gets off the dead and desensitised surface of the reader's mind, and onto a part that will register' (GK, 51). It works by much the same means of contiguity as the Image, but is Vorticism's 'ACTIVE pattern. . . that sets things in motion' (PE, 51) and of course provides for an unlimited number of relevant units of meaning – or, rather, for a psychological rather than formal climax, in that ideogrammic structure is completed at the instant when it functions, when the flash of comprehension occurs.[40] The ideogram is not just a poetic technique, it is an educational and psychological principle.

The basis of Pound's theory is his view that the human reason works by making what he called 'illogical' inductive leaps from the observation of isolated facts to a general inclusive perception of a system of thought, general rule, or truth-model (ABC, 19-23; GK, 51-2/*passim*). Fenollosa's exposition of the Chinese written character is a model for a similar inductive process.[41] Pound's view of this process is based on a belief that it requires merely a sensible study of detail for it to function. Objectivity and the lack of discursive description can be seen as a kind of guarantee that the process will 'work': the naked juxtaposition of detail, and the consequential inductive leap, will overcome stock responses, or social clichés, and reinforce the individual basis of understanding by literally forcing the subject who is perceiving to rebuild, or make new that whole truth of which the poet or critic or teacher has given significant elements. Theory is an individual formulation, made by piling up concrete examples into a kind of accretive justification. Pound regarded this inductive method as particularly scientific (ABC, 26). His appeal to scientific method[42] was obviously motivated by a desire to establish a way in which poetical and critical methods could assume a 'scientific' status of verifiability. He seems never to have been aware of the central objection to inductive logic posed by a range of philosophers from David Hume to Karl Popper, that no finite number of examples is ever enough to guarantee an absolutely truthful universal principle. In a sense, however, all Pound's talk of the scientific basis of induction is a red herring. What the ideogrammic constation does of course establish is not an unfalsifiable theory, but a psychological expectation. And his true concern was with the psychological act of understanding, grasping and subjectivising knowledge. The true implication of ideogrammic theory lies in an approach to an *act of imagining* undertaken by the reader; the purpose of writing is to reveal, and of reading, to achieve an active understanding (GK, 51). The true analogy is not to scientific induction but to the act of fusion in the creative imagination.

The ideogrammic concept ignores sequential or causal principles of

120

discourse. In this it resembles, and may through Hulme have been influenced by, Henri Bergson's 'intensive manifold'. Hulme wrote[43] of synthesising complexes of literary language in relation to asyntactical expression; syntax was seen as an extensive manifold, and poetry – being an intensive mode – was independent of it. On the other hand, Pound's ideogram is in part inconsistent with its most obvious source. It was presumably Fenollosa's monograph, *The Chinese written character as a medium for poetry*, which gave Pound not only the name for his cluster or 'constatation', but also the basic accretive analogy for the putting together of details. Pound probably received the essay in the Fenollosa material he was given late in 1913; it was available to him during the period of Vorticism, and like Pound's own vorticist essays, develops an aesthetic argument by means of a series of visual analogies. However, Fenollosa's argument stresses the importance to poetry of strong transitive verbs;[44] he insists on the value of a poetic syntax based on the transfer of force from agent to object, and at first Pound emphasised the importance of this element (Letters, 82). However he was more lastingly concerned with the structure of the single ideograph, or image-sign, which he followed Fenollosa in considering to be pictorial. The Chinese character as Fenollosa and Pound both took it is made up of a number of elements which are formalised pictures of things, and the ideograph is the sum of those concrete elements: its significance is inductively achieved from the conjunction of a number of conceptually-related 'real' things. The important thing is that the juxtaposed particulars are not *accidental*. Juxtaposition expresses their true relationship, and the relationship must therefore be seen as their *meaning*. Each ideograph presents the reader not just with an ultimate import, but with the factual data which, gathered, gave rise to that import; linguistically, each of the characters contains within it the historical contexts in which is has evolved and been used: its own etymology.[45] It is in this second sense that the ideograph resembles the instantaneous, asyntactical logopoeic complex. Here, as Pound said, 'a new mode of thought was foeseen' (PE, 51) with all the intensive qualities of concreteness and condensation. There is no doubt that he was drawn to Fenollosa's essay because of its assertion that the Chinese method of notation was a natural presentation of reality corresponding most directly to nature. Pound therefore emphasised its factual message and described the essay as a basis for an aesthetic (Letters, 106).

It is of course well known that the pictographs of Fenollosa's essay are more like a shorthand code; some of the elements which Fenollosa and Pound interpreted literally are actually only conventional sound symbols and determinates. However this is irrelevant to an understanding of the aesthetic system which Pound based on them.[46] Fenollosa described a representation of reality analogous to verbal etymology,

121

rather than a conventionalised code, and therefore 'we do not seem to be juggling mental counters, but to be watching things work out their fate'.[47] Pound accepted the view of the ideograph as a uniquely intensive presentation of concrete reality. He was aware that the method was unorthodox,[48] but its effect seemed to be to relate the ideogram and the Image, and he was always eager for additional evidence to support his existing aesthetic arguments.

The essence of ideogrammic theory, at least for Pound, lay in a construction of a complex of signifying words which may be anything from the name of a quality or physical entity to a formal Image, or 'intellectual and emotional complex', placed in a relationship which excludes all manner of transitional connecting structures, so that the units are explained only by the fact of their juxtaposition, not by causal or discursive means. The effect, which is cumulative, is similar in both prose and poetry, although Pound may have considered that the units were more carefully arranged, and therefore more intensive, in poetry (LE, 26). The nature of the relationship between one unit and another and within the ideogram as a whole is left to the reader's understanding. It is in fact the *essential* meaning which he must grasp by a process of inductive logic: meaning consubstantial with the form of the whole. That understanding or intellectual penetration is achieved suddenly and energetically, as in the case of the Image: it is in fact in this extended sense that a long poem or a Noh play can be called an Image (GB, 109*n*). Equally, the ideogram must be so precisely presented in every detail, so authoritative, and so charged with emotion as to achieve a unity equivalent to an insight reaching into all its elements. It is no simple association of things for a predetermined purpose but, like the Vortex, an experimental, energetic product of the conceiving intellect.[49] The ideogram focuses within the gaps of language. It resists closure, having no inclusive, consistent, closed meaning. The ideogram can forever include additional elements and relations within its pattern; but it closes in the specific psychological or performative sense of attaining completeness at the instant when it flashes into the reader's understanding, when the unrelated elements join and the association springs into full life and significance.[50] The ideogram which is thus formed is a representation of the poet's own knowledge; but because of the ellipses of discourse, it is a knowledge which Pound believed to be communicated in an unbiassed and peculiarly truthful manner. Thus perceived, the ideogrammic system is the product of Pound's old concern to find an ultimate poetic sincerity. It is pattern removed from the privacy of an author's perceptions and seen instead as catalyst for the reader's perception of the truth. The author therefore assists the reader by manipulating the reading pattern, including all its formal elements even to the layout and typography of the printed page, until that unitary end arises (LE, 441). This is creative thought; it supersedes Aristotelian logic.

This understanding of Pound's ideogrammic theory will clarify the nature and meaning of the transitional poems. The problem posed by the structure of 'Near Perigord', with its various truth-statements all of equal weight and validity and its summation in the image of the broken mirror, is answered by the juxtaposition of various truths and the failure to discover a single truth in terms of closure of the text (although the third section with its reminiscence of conventional poetic closures seems to offer this without involving the conventional discursive narrative which we would expect of such a closure). Similarly, *Mauberley*: it is as though Pound were laying out a series of counters, giving us this image and this and this and this, through the complex movements of the whole sequence, in the expectation that by the final addition of the 'Medallion' poem the reader will achieve an inductive leap to a truth which is not contained in, or expressed by, 'Medallion', but is in the fact that the unit of 'Medallion' has joined the other elements of the sequence, each word, Image, stanza, poem, each section of the whole. The meaning of *Hugh Selwyn Mauberley* is constructed of those units, their relationships, and the associations brought to the poem by the reader reading. It is only achieved within his mind.

The explication of the ideogrammic method, and its exemplification, are to be found in Pound's last prose book of any length, and the only one he wrote after *The spirit of romance*: his *Guide to kulchur* (1938). In its subject and approach, *Kulchur* appears to be a sequel to 'How to read' (1929) and *ABC of reading* (1934), but its range has been extended to include cultural documents beyond the range of Pound's high-literary tradition, and it moves beyond his concern with the level of linguistic technique. Its avowed aim is to assist the formulation of moral action in society rather than literary action, composition. Yet the book remains the work of a man whose values are aesthetic rather than 'historical' in any normal sense. It is not the fact itself or how it has been arrived at which interests Pound here: it is what can be built from the facts which will be of lasting value in the culture.[51] It is from this point that the writer of the *Cantos* set out on his voyage after knowledge (GK, 294).

Kulchur is one of Pound's most openly didactic works, as well as the prose most clearly related, in its sources and themes, to the early Cantos. Its strategy is to represent the state of Pound's knowledge as it developed over a period of two months in 1937. It functions as a heuristic tool, setting out to stimulate the reader's enquiry into relations between, and analogies for, a number of historical facts, both literary and social. Except the *Cantos* itself, this was Pound's most extreme attempt to break down academic categories, to deny the values of

123

specialisation, and to survey an inclusive range of knowledge.

Pound's argument moves abruptly from one unit to the next, seeking the inductive moment of synthesis. Thus for instance in the chapter called 'Tradition', Pound set out to define civilisation by a sequence of four numbered sub-sections, announcing an ideogrammic strategy (GK, 80-4). The first describes 'Listening to incense' at the Imperial Japanese court, an exercise in associating elements of scents with poetry in a 'blend of perception and association' evidencing sensitivity and education; the second contains anecdotal references to the Chinese court and Fenollosa's Noh, comparing one play with specific Homeric elements; the third provides a contrasting set of personal allusions to the witness of Pound's generation to the collapse of contemporary European cultures, all equally decadent: 'They had no moral splendour'; and the last contains anecdotes of meetings in artists' studios in Paris. The chapter is excessively self-conscious, as this outline must suggest, and its ideogrammic purity is marred by Pound's loss of nerve, for after all he cannot be certain that his nondiscursive strategy is clear, and apart from more unconscious moments of identifications, he included three italicised passages in which he could explain his purpose:

'I am not merely taking a pot shot . . . , I am contrasting the fine flower of a civilisation with a species of rot and corruption.'
' . . . I am not in these slight memories merely "pickin' daisies." A man does not know his own ADDRESS (in time) until he knows where his time and milieu stand in relation to other times and conditions.'
' . . . In attempting to discover "where in a manner of speaking etc we have got to . . . " . . . one can use allegory or date, trifling or grave things seen. . . . ' (GK, 82-4)

Speaking for myself — and with the ideogrammic method it may be impossible to speak for anyone else — I do not need these explanations, for the conjunction is as meaningful without them. However, the ideogrammic disclaimers have the unintended advantage of making the strategy much clearer than a wholly successful ideogram might have done. The air of improvisation, always hanging about this method, is emphasised by the comments. As allusive as a poem, *Kulchur* can be seen as a vast ideogram containing units of reference to cultural fact, document, and event; in most places it does leave to the reader the task of synthesising the presented detail and forming inductive conclusions which are the 'meaning' of the book.

This ideogrammic mode is not only highly allusive; it is extremely dependent on memory and association, primarily Pound's own memory and associations. It is ironic that this is so. In 1933 Pound had written that the ideogrammic method 'must be applied in the making of text books *all along the line*' in order to confront the student with the facts.

124

Objective truth. The problem lies in a solipsistic confusion between himself and the reader or other, the subject in whose mind the ideogram must spring to conclusion. Believing, with the anthropologist Frobenius, that 'It is not what a man says but the part of it which his auditor considers important that determines the amount of communication'.[52] Pound sought to make the reader accompany him from one significant detail to the next, until they leap together to the intellectual synthesis contained in their relationship. Where Pound seems to have miscalculated is in the nature of the facts he presents. The author is very present in passages like that which I described above. The facts or details are presented in terms of personal significance, almost of reminiscence — subjective associations. The important thing for Pound's heuristic purpose is that the synthesis be personally accomplished. And yet we have seen him *assuring his reader that he has made a synthesis* — that the 'active instant and present awareness' which is personal wisdom (GK, 51-2, 28) has been truthfully accomplished: 'It is my intention in this book to COMMIT myself on as many points as possible' (GK, 7). He will GIVE us that part of knowledge which he considers important; he even tries to complete 'this new Vade Mecum without opening other volumes, I am to put down so far as possible only what has resisted the erosion of time, and forgetfulness' (GK, 33). The ideogrammic method might be giving us a rain of data; but in fact that turns out to be an account of achieved meaning. Pound advises us against academic learning in the sense of opinion drawn from other people's facts (GK, 29) only to give us himself making an entirely idiosyncratic revelation of the materials by which his own critical experience was formed, and actually falling into discursive descriptions of what is happening and why, while still (necessarily, given the breadth of his references) omitting the full chronological detail of the process which would complete the logical ellipses of the book. What we have now is a new mimesis, a reflection of a moment of the author's mind.

Great intellectual control is required to relate concrete references (a term, an idea, an image, a book or a phrase) to others in a way which leaves those terms *and* their original context distinct and at the same time synthesised in a mutual clarification. What is unclear, in *Guide to kulchur*, is that Pound had actually expended the time and the conscious care to control his objective pattern or constatation of facts in the way that he intended. Ideogrammic theory proposes that both the power of the synthesis *and* the importance of the elements used should validate the whole. 'Direct treatment of the thing' becomes more important than ever, in prose as in verse, although that 'thing' may now be a whole literary text; principles of objectivity and linguistic precision are of the greatest importance. Yet time and time again, Pound sank into the didacticism which time and time again he had rejected. We are told that we 'ought to "appreciate" ', 'oughtn't to think', 'ought NOT to be a blighted haystack of knowledge . . .' (Indeed not.)

The ideogram OUGHT, then, to work in the purity and objectivity of juxtapositions and relationships. It fails when it falls into directives based on the quirky didacticism of the subjective author. 'Ideas are true as they go into action. I am not resurrecting a pragmatic sanction, but trying to light up a pragmatic PROOF' (GK, 188) Pound said: and forgot himself.

Discourse and form: starting to read the Cantos

> 'the verb is "see", not "walk on"
> ie it coheres all right
> even if my notes do not cohere.' (*Cantos*, 116/797)

Pound's *Cantos*, like his *Guide to Kulchur*, is ideogrammic: an encyclopaedic, new, 'totalitarian' (GK, 95) synthesis. It is not merely an ideogrammic poem, but an ideogram, a guide to culture communicating its meaning in a constatation of material facts of all kinds. Of the various accounts of the poem which Pound offered on occasions to friends, family and readers it is worth pointing out that as early as 1917 it was projected as 'endless' (Letters, 157); that by 1922 the first eleven cantos could be thought of as 'preparation of the palette' containing the elements to be used in the poem but not in 'some sort of design' (Letters, 247); and that in 1932 he categorised its content as simply 'the permanent, the recurrent, the casual' (Letters, 321). Among those material facts are the historical (Pound called epic a 'poem including history' LE, 86), autobiographical, traditional and mythical; its methods are allusive and associational in the way that 'Near Perigord' or *Hugh Selwyn Mauberley* is, but of course with a more extensive material and temporal range which is placed in contiguity. Probably the *Cantos* should be thought of as a kind of ideal inclusivity. Its constituents involve not only the historical categories listed, but all possible ways of including them such as examples, translations, literary references like quotations and adaptations, criticism, comparison of texts, 'excernment' by selection and juxtaposition, and the logopoeic manipulation of diction to illuminate meaning by verbal associations, adaptations, stylistic imitations, dialect, colloquialism, and the high literary, Latinate style. The search for meaning in the *Cantos* is the search for a map of knowledge: a voyage ranging through time and space as they exist in language and in a cultural tradition.

It has been argued convincingly that when Pound abandoned the first published 'Ur-Cantos' and started again with the Homeric materials of the present Canto 1, he did so as a result of discovering James Joyce's *Ulysses*, with its intellectual and associational voyage through tradition

126

and language.[53] Yet the basis for a voyage of this kind had been established by Pound years before — in 1910, when he described the structure of Dante's *Divine comedy* in terms of a journey which was simultaneously literal, a journey through states of mind, a symbol of a struggle for understanding, and an image of laws of justice (SR, 127). Of course the *Commedia* is unified by the literal level, the causal narrative structure. It possesses a plot, a linear history to which a variety of incidents and perceptions has been attached. Furthermore, that narrative line is conventionally identified by a number of directives, especially by the authorial strategy of an actor-narrator whose perceptions and personality offer a guarantee of truth-telling.

By comparison, Pound's 'Ur-Cantos' debate the possibility of finding such an authorial strategy for his project. The poet, who is identified by his colloquial and subjectivised discourse, speaks of searching for a subject and form, rather like Wordsworth at the opening of the *Prelude* debating the validity of human language and the viability of an autobiography of the imagination. Pound asks[53] how he can make a poem that will conform to his subjective experience, and what figures will represent his own life, imaginatively extended in being and time. He implies that the poem must be subjective and expressive, and suggests that his personal Virgil could be Robert Browning — an aesthetic guide through the dark wood of expression, who had 'had the form' for self-expression; but Pound feels that Browning had written in a less fragmented age than his own, and had therefore been able to use the authorial *persona* of Sordello in the then-new form of the meditative, semi-dramatic, semi-epic narrative poem. It was therefore Browning's example as a discoverer of new and specific discourse, rather than his precise expressive form, which was available to Pound; to follow Browning's dramatic monologues makes use of the simplest authorial stance. When Pound advances the problem of finding a different but equally expressive combination of form and author, he is actually suggesting that Browning's method is not now reusable — although he continued to play with the possibility of discovering some different but similar author; a number of possibilities is named, from Bertran de Born and Uc St. Circ, to Hueffer and Yeats.

Pound discussed his 'Ur-Cantos' at some point with T S Eliot, who later recorded his view of them as an 'objective and reticent autobiography' and the 'final fusion' of all Pound's *personae*.[55] Yet any examination of the texts must conclude that Eliot was writing of Pound's unaltered intentions rather than his achievement to date. His abandonment of the authorial alternative was inevitable when he arrived at a view of himself as sitting at the point of a vortex, a node of perception of different consciousnesses (especially those of poetic forebears), and as reaching to a beginning whose form in fact evaded him for another

127

five years. 'You have no cosmos till you can order it', as he admitted; and 'I fail, I fail, stumbling.' His first version of Canto IV therefore crumbles into a 'phantastikon' or kaleidescope of moments of experience which snap sharply from one to the next, like the swift horizontal wipes of the silent films. 'Ur-Cantos' V, VI and VII waver between the objective and the authorial; but by the completion of the revisions of this material for the extant published version, certain structural possibilities were at last abandoned.

Of Pound's various descriptions or explanations of the *Cantos*, none has entirely satisfied its readers. A number of references to it as an epic, or 'tale of the tribe', comparable to the epic *Divine comedy*,[56] seem to represent one major view which Pound cared to promote. However it evades an essential difficulty in approaching the poem: it is historical and representational, or mythical and symbolic, or expressionist? In structure, or organisation of materials, the poem in any case does not approximate the epic in any way which seems very helpful, and indeed readers were misled for decades, by the expectation of a final *paradiso*, to look for a simple moral format. As far as a structure is concerned, Pound's statements seem to suggest something very long and without a generic form: a 'chryselephantine poem of immeasurable length', 'Phanopoeia or something or other, all about everything . . .'[57] His early titles for them — *A draft of XVI cantos* (1925), *A draft of the cantos: 17-27* (1928) and *A draft of XXX cantos* (1930) — mirror this uncertainty and suggest that at least until 1930 Pound imagined that the kind of revisions he had made for the beginning of the published version might continue over some period of time. By the time that he had been working on the poem for a decade or so, however, Pound had discovered the apparent description of his structure as a 'fugue'; this is what he informed W B Yeats, who mentions it in *A vision*, and also his father: 'Rather like, or unlike subject and response and counter subject in fugue' (Letters, 285). Aside from the verbal hesitation here, it could be pointed out that when Pound continued, in this letter of 1927, to try to elaborate the statement, his explanation rapidly became nothing more than a descriptive catalogue of contents in the order in which they appear. In any case, the fugal structure cannot be traced in any strict sense, and it seems the term means little more than a recurrence of thematic elements; that this occurs is obvious; how and why, less so. What Pound's references to categories of content — for example the permanent, the recurrent, the casual[58] — actually indicate is a discourse arising out of its own linguistic necessities. It is not possible to read the work as a realistic narrative in which Pound, as author, somehow withholds information which he intends eventually to reveal, and so end the work. His various attempts to explain the *Cantos* sometimes sound teasing, as though he is maintaining a deliberate reticence, like the writer

128

of a murder mystery refusing to reveal the guilty party. Yet the rhetorical impatience of something like his 1927 letter to his father (Letters, 284-6) is, I think, most likely to be an impatience with himself and an inability to describe detail in abstract categories. The question which must be asked is whether, in a text like the *Cantos*, the poet himself could ever be fully aware of the 'truth' he promises?[59]

As to content, the materials of history (presented strikingly by means of literary documentation and allusion to things 'held in the memory') fill the categories of repeated patterns and unrepeated pattern-units. The meaning of the *Cantos* can be sought here, among units connected by recurring, echoing allusive images, with every recurrence bringing into the ideogrammic whole, all previous contexts. What the *Cantos* does not contain, in terms of an epic, is of course a narrative in the sense of an Aristotelian action with a beginning, middle and end, and a sequence of temporal and logical causality. The appearance and reappearance of certain actions presented anecdotally tends to create a readerly expectation of narrative. Put simply, we *expect* a fiction of such length to possess a plot. But this expectation is constantly defeated by means of ideogrammic juxtaposition. The materials of the poem are established in a linear mode only in the sense that a printed text implies some physical linearity, the reading from left to right and top to bottom of the page (in our culture) — from beginning to end: from a beginning to an end which, in the present case, means from page three to page 797. However, just as the syntax is disturbed by logopoeic and ideogrammic methodology, so is the relationship between units of content. Even within a single page, the content occurs and the meaning thence arises according to a kind of *gestalt*, a falling-into-place in the act of reading of all the elements of expression and significance.

For many readers it appears that this *gestalt* event does not happen, so that the poem retains an 'evasive, centreless quality'[60] and contiguity remains *merely* contiguity, and accidental. Most readers would agree that sections of the work possess their unity denied to the whole. Of the most clearly-unified sections of sequences, two — the Chinese history cantos 52 to 61 and the American history cantos 62 to 71 — possess a unity which depends not only on the reproduction of a documentary source, but on the consistency of the way in which the sources are used. These two sequences consist of quotation-allusions, selected and reproduced in a linear order, from a very extensive original document: in the first case, de Mailla's *Histoire générale de la Chine* (Paris, 1777-83), and in the second Charles F Adams's edition of *The works of John Adams* (Boston, 1850). Examinations of the notebooks which Pound used when he was constructing these sections[61] reveals that he worked by copying out brief passages as he read through the source, placing them into a poetic typography in the order of the

129

source, usually verbally unaltered, and normally free of any authorial comment or summary, and certainly of any interpretation. Because Pound built the documentation into the canto at hand without altering the order of the source, the Adams cantos follow the editor's selection rather than historical chronology. Pound's failure to re-order his selections is in a sense a refusal to suggest that meaning could be expressed by a diachronic or causal structure. He is refusing to supply what could be thought of as a subjective interpretation of the construct. By doing so he is failing to include history in one sense, for the status of his documentation is such that it possesses a secondary significance: what is being alluded to in the poem is not Chinese history, but Mailla's history (interpretation, presentation and structuring of fact). Or, as the ordering of the Adams materials makes even clearer, not John Adams himself, but his grandson's version of Adams's life and times. The 'author' of these sequences is on one level Pound, the selector and amanuensis, and on another and more direct level, a second writer whose relationship to his material is not unlike Pound's to Propertius in the *Homage*.

Pound developed his methodology in the 1920s. As he worked on the 'drafts' of the first thirty cantos he was also preparing his edition of *Guido Cavalcanti: rime*. In doing so he visited a number of Italian libraries, jotting down bibliographical notes, translations of phrases, lines: apparently he moved from one manuscript to another, seeking to clarify textual obscurities, but paying no special attention to the priority of one version over another.[62] The same mixture of notes, quoted phrases and translation is found in the text of the *Cantos* as early as the 'Malatesta' sequence (Cantos, 8/28 to 11/52), and by the mid-thirties, in the fullest and most rapid flow of writing, Pound had extended the method. The *Fifth decad of cantos* (1937) has already fully developed the strategy of objective documentation. A characteristic early draft of the last three pages of Canto 43, for instance, which is dated 1936,[63] suggests that Pound was lifting such material directly from the source book, omitting some duplicated or excessively extended stuff and shortening some phraseology. In revision, he cut parts of the prose scribbled into the notebooks, working rhythmically at the lines as he altered them, especially avoiding the iambic foot. But what is remarkable in the *Poetry notebooks* of the 1930s is the extent to which basic sources move unaltered through revisions into the published text, where they sit, authentic and unsupported by any descriptive or 'writerly' material.

Of course the draft versions are not entirely quoted, or notational, material. Pound breaks in very occasionally with a subjective comment: interestingly this is *less* frequent in the published text than in the earlier drafts. In early versions of Canto 61, for instance, a marginal note reads: "Natus J. Adams"; and as Pound finished de Mailla and Canto 51, he

130

noted[64] that the poem must go back in time — a reference to historical linearity; but these do not appear in the published text. If the author does not appear, *an* author sometimes does, however tangentially. An example is the dialect speech which is identified by a semi-phonetic spelling in Canto 62 (Cantos, 62/342) especially of the *editor*'s name, where there is a curious identification thus of a commentator on the text, and a personality within Pound's discourse. Although this happens briefly, it creates a momentary author who can be defined as 'the-person-who-speaks-thus'.[65] It is not the 'author' which is the Adams *Works*, for they are written in a standard educated English of the period, as in the overt quotation on the previous page, and more generally throughout the section. The dialect creates a problem, for in a sense it should not exist and its effect is to disturb the authorial, documentary unity of the sequence as regularly established and to jolt the reader out of a stylistic expectation. It is a defamiliarising effect; but its purpose is unclear.

A second kind of unity, and different from that of any other sequence since the rejected 'Ur-Cantos', comes with the *Pisan cantos*. The sequence possesses a subjective, lyric unity. The text is given its closure by the strategy of autobiographical references. It is as though here at last, in this section, Pound has reverted to the single author of his early expressive poetry, the purposeful author abandoned in the divisions of *Hugh Selwyn Mauberley*. (It is significant that the present author dreams of the London to which *Mauberley* bade farewell.) Allusions are grouped around Pound's experience; the author is memory with a cluster of associations, his stream-of-consciousness. That the associations *are* personal is witnessed by the coded nature of their obscurity, and by the student's recognition that they are representational, for there are anecdotal references to people and events in the public realms of Pound's life, as well as clearly nostalgic references to materials in earlier *Cantos* and an elegiac tone which gives those references a stylistic coherence. This complex of allusion and association creates its own significance consistent with that of the *Cantos* as a whole — a cluster of cultural and aesthetic values which are permanent in, and at the same time independent of, historical time and place. The tone of the Pisan sequence is more consistent than that of any other, its author-validated truth-statements clearer and less dependent on implicit or accidental understandings, and buttressed by interpretative statements expressed with all the authoritative power of a language rich in imagistic and rhythmical energies, bringing in their own associations drawn from the traditions of valid art, of great art:

> 'What thou lovest well remains,
> the rest is dross
> What thou lov's well shall not be reft from thee. . . .

> The ant's a centaur in his dragon world.
> Pull down thy vanity. . . . '   (Cantos, 81/521)

It would be wrong to suggest that the *Pisan* sequence works consistently in this fashion; certainly, despite similar passages elsewhere, the *Cantos* as a whole does not. *Thrones* and *Rock drill*, powerful as their statement is, move back from both the unity of the Chinese and American Cantos, and that of the Pisan, into a more elliptical discourse, one which presents an ideogrammic strategy in still more trying circumstances. Cantos 85 and 86, for example, quote a number of Chinese ideographs which the normal Western reader can neither hear nor understand. They are elements of discourse which remain a coded symbol. They allude to Chinese material (structurally, to Chinese material in the preceding Cantos), therefore they are signifiers of an ethical system. The marginalia in the text refers to Couvreur's *Chou king*. [66] Essentially, the ideographs function as allusions by pulling the Chinese text after them into the signified meaning of these Cantos.

Most of the text of *Rock drill* and *Thrones* operates on this level of difficulty. Much of the material is allusively subjective, like the *Pisan cantos*; but now the allusions are shorter and more rapid, more notational, and often refer to a fuller usage in an earlier Canto, so that the text is folded in upon itself in an increasingly complex self-signifying linguistic system.

Allusiveness, if not so intensive a manifestation of it, is typical of Cantos discourse as of related poems like *Propertius* and *Mauberley*. The mode functions throughout the text, whatever the nature or source of the material which is in this way being incorporated into its codes. There is a more culturally assimilated example of this allusiveness in Canto 7, a poem closely analogous to the transitional poems, dealing with their theme of the enduring validity of the emotion which can be adequately formulated in art, but which is also reasonably typical of the methodology of the first fifty-one cantos. Canto 7 deals with both the subjective and traditional experience. It contains allusions to the Beauty which is signified by the literary-Aphrodite figure of Eleanor, Homer's Helen, Pound's Ione, and Liu Che's 'dead leaf': physical beauty given the immortal embodiment of art. These women form a complex of allusions associated with cultural values which in turn are associated with poets of creative *virtù* − Homer, Ovid, Dante, the Troubadours, Pound himself. The significance of the whole relationship is the way in which Art is the means of giving impermanent physical beauty a form and context outlasting time − time as tradition, as human life, as the old men ('Dry casques of departed locusts') and society (imaged in the historically-degenerated physical details of imitation marble, 'modish and darkish walls' and the statue beside the

132

machined symmetry of a beer bottle (Cantos, 7/24-7).) The allusion forms a complex which does not merely set the twentieth century against the past, although such a juxtaposition does include much detail; it sets up the relationship between the thing which is 'in time', subject to decay, and the thing which is in the memory, formed art, 'Passion to breed a form in a shimmer of rain-blur . . .' (Cantos, 7/25)[67] This relationship is reminiscent of both T S Eliot's *Waste land* with its own 'dryness calling for death' (Cantos, 7/26) and its conjunction of time and memory, and of *Mauberly*. Its objective detail functions, not in a digressive discourse but by the accretion of significant references into a patterned complex. 'These fragments you have shelved/shored', as the text so ambiguously proposes, moving the first elements of the canto from the waste land of contemporary London and Paris, to the fields of Renaissance Italy, art against art, war set against war.

Canto 7 can be seen as one of Pound's more consistent fusions of a variety of critical allusions into a meaningful 'constatation'. Allusions to recurring or permanent traditional units of meaning are the elements of constatation; this is the recurrence of the poem, not merely in things like the references and anecdotes of Canto 7, but in the Chaucerian adaptations of the first lines of Canto 30; or the whole of the Usura Canto, 45, whose meaning is significantly contained within its rhythmical, repetitive verbal patterns alluding to the King James *Bible*; or the references to English Renaissance poetry in the *Pisan cantos*; or the musical text of Canto 75 with its song of Arnaut Daniel enduring through time and loss, made-new in Münch's modern setting. The 'meaning' of such materials lies only partly in their simple discourses. It is equally, or more, in the reader's recognition of the signifying nature of the materials to hand. And that recognition comes only through the establishment of patterns of relationship. Before long, the *Cantos* become self-referential; the allusions are to its own discourse.

Pound's objectivity, which is based on respect for the integrity or special, truth-telling nature of allusion, remains perhaps too non-discursive for many readers. Where allusions of all kinds are juxtaposed with the purpose of revealing, in contiguity, both their latent significance and that of all other units of signification simultaneously, then the text remains open. There is never any single, ultimate interpretation. The reader cannot be certain of knowing just what limited meaning inheres in the individual image, what are the boundaries of the meaning which it carries into the ideogram. If we take a random example of the American history cantos, we can see that here the ideogrammic strategy requires the *objective* insertion of material into the text. That material however must be looked at as both objective and symbolic; for Pound, the 'natural object is always the adequate symbol' (LE, 5, 9). Readers who are familiar with the detail of the *Cantos* will possess some awareness of the self-referential pattern which is being evolved; but it may not be practicable in all cases to understand the full intentional meaning of the object, given that it carries with it − 'symbolises' − not just other objects, but abstract relationships. Occasionally Pound does reveal what an object means for him personally; but the ideogrammic method removes both author and subjective validation from most areas of the poem. In this kind of poem, we cannot fully know meaning. We may know a meaning, our meaning, because reading is a form of experience.

The *Cantos* is incapable of interpretation because of both local complexities and a problem of the form of the whole. The former is the more striking, perhaps. An extreme instance of the problem can be seen in Hugh Kenner's description[68] of Pound's intended final canto, which was to include sixteen Chinese ideograms, blocked into four lines of four, a Chinese quatrain consisting of 'the sixteen ideograms I find most interesting', with notes on their pronunciation. In theory this should 'make-new' a set of terms, Pound's favourite signs, in context. For any probable reader, however, their simple denotation is lacking. What remains? Not an authorial interpretation, describing their significance. Perhaps an allusion to a meaning-cluster which includes all the previous contexts for the appearance of the signs; or perhaps the *fact* that they are Chinese and are therefore a form of trans-cultural, contextually moral, signification; or perhaps more, since even at the end of his writing Pound was asserting his belief in the existence of an independent truth, although he no longer believed that his ideogram adequately signified it: 'ie it coheres all right / even if my notes do not cohere' (Cantos, 116/797).

And that of course is the problem of the form of the whole. Readers are accustomed to a kind of discourse which defines itself and limits its boundaries by conventional representational and structural devices. Pound's strategy is intensely defamiliarising in its effect; we react by assuming that some element of meaning has been omitted and try to remedy this by supplying mimetic references for what we have. In the case of Canto 85, already mentioned, Pound's juxtaposed quotations seem unable to support the meaning of the passage, and his explanatory footnotes result from an unspoken recognition of the fact, which is the fact of the failure of his form to coalesce. This canto is making a statement about Couvreur's content and style; but it is an *authored* statement, an opinion rather than a constatation. There are many less obvious examples of this. Therefore, although parts of the *Cantos* attain a partial truth, others remain accidental, like an anthology of quotations on various topics. Pound's purpose is clear: to create a total constatation independent of chronology or cultural boundaries, and donative to artistic tradition. But the openness of his method, which his
134

theory so clearly called for and his practice recognised, leaves meaning eternally indeterminate. Methods of textual criticism may occasionally help toward an understanding of a meaning in which references and relationships, statement and form, are coterminous, but in the last analysis these cannot cope with ideogrammic method, because detail must be interpreted in order for the context to be understood, and the context, for the detail. An example of the problem is the way in which critics have interpreted the reference to Aphrodite at the end of Canto 1. The translation of Andreas Divus's lines (Cantos 1/5) has usually been seen as signifying an inferior, degenerate art because of their overly-formalised rhetoric.[67] But George Dekker, in considering the weight of the Aphrodite theme throughout the *Cantos*, has pointed out that these lines are the first, and therefore inevitably important, appearance of the goddess of creative passion, a very positive being in the poem's terms. It seems impossible to accept either judgement, if this requires a rejection of the other. In the context of the work, both seem equally truthful.

So that the nature of the poetic discourse which is the *Cantos* has frequently been misunderstood. Readers expect to be able to interpret Pound's so-called 'epic' in the narrative and representational terms appropriate to the genre, explaining each element by reference either to cause and effect, or to what someone in the poem convincingly says about it, or by its reference, mimetic or analogous, to the real, physical world. All this was Pound's fault: his friendly explanations of a fugal analogy, or comparisons with Dante's moral system, and even his very understandable assumption that there *is* a pre-existing truth which he would eventually manage to communicate by the achieved form of the whole work — all these are references to a *closed* text. The proposals which are implicit in the poem itself, and specifically explained in Pound's prose, that an aim is to teach the reader excernmentally by sending him to significant source materials, suggests a meaning enclosed in those materials and existing outside the poem itself, as though the whole work were merely another of these student syllabuses he used to draw up. In fact, the status of the document sources seems rather different: it may be that we should think of them as being, like the *Cantos* too, parts of the great text of language: that the material from, for instance, Mailla, which is not actually quoted, should be thought of as ideally present within the ellipses of the text: that it is merely one of the various Absences in the text, implicit in the unverbalised relationships or energies of the work.

For the same reason, the text's emphasis on history is misleading. The existence of independent, authoritative historical fact is irrelevant; meaning is in the implicit relationship between history and other kinds of experience. The *Cantos* may 'include' history, but it is *myth*: unveri-

135

fiable, unfalsifiable hypothesis, like the ideogram itself. Pound sought to create an artifact vibrant in its relations, a vortex of meaning. If Pound says that 'We also made ghostly visits, and the stair / That knew us, found us again on the turn of it' (Cantos 7/25) then the allusion is fused with the significant situation, the author's perception of it, and the cultural context. The essence of the achievement is the illumination of a situation, not the original, factual purity of the reference: we are not being asked to identify a real staircase.

The *Cantos* is the final, most extensive ideogram, constatation of facts, 'factual rain' of details. Structurally it is like the Image – an extended Image which holds within it the intensive complex of material elements in the implicit relationships of a vast system of associations. Its goal, like that of the Image, is an achieved complex of language, sensuous and conceptual, which depends for its effectiveness on achieving an imaginative event in the imagination of the reader. Theoretically, th ultimate poem now exists only in the reader's mind. Truth is not something told, but something perceived.

Perhaps the ideogram was too much contaminated by Pound's old belief in Longinian illumination, that moment of ecstatic transport so much more important than the formal shape of the poem. There is a fundamental, inescapable refusal of closure in ideogrammic practice; but Pound sought to deny this by defining the act of closure in terms of the creation of illumination in its fusion. Pound's *Cantos* form probably the longest poem to be written in accordance with a structural principle which holds immeasurable numbers of details in a non-discursive, and partly non-verbal, relationship. It is, however, by no means the only poem to function so; for it is of the nature of Modernism to hold detail in a selective, non-representational pattern. The vast ideogram of the *Cantos* is essentially a didactic edifice intended to work in the mind of its readers to produce a unique imaginative structure: the illumination of the object, and simultaneously of the subject, of imagination. As we have seen, non-ideogrammic structures exist within sections of the work: the History cantos, the *Pisan cantos*, and to some extent in the first thirty cantos as a whole because blocks of recurring themes and images create a comparatively unified statement. But if the poem as a whole possesses any structure, that most resembles what Pound had perceived in some kind of novels, Jamesian masses in opposition, Joycean correspondences, rather than either the fluid or the symmetrical forms of his earlier theory.

In any other sense, too much has been left to the reader. This is poetry backwards, a theory of the reader writing the poem. But to understand it may begin to provide a strategy for reading the *Cantos* which depends on recognising a sequence of truth-statements and the nature of the unparaphrasable truths which they state.

136

The essence of the open, readerly text is to be contradictory, disturbing. The remarkable thing about Pound's Vorticist, logopoeic theories is their implicit perception of this decades before post-Saussurean literary theorists formulated it. And from it, the nature of the *Cantos* can be understood: a didactic, disturbing and demanding multi-dimensional text requiring its readers to undergo a process involving the entire reception of the Poundian system. And yet what Pound appears not to have seen is that for every reader of an open text there is a truth, for a plurality of readers, a plurality of meanings. *This* truth is neither single nor reassuring.

NOTES

I THE SPIRIT OF ROMANTICISM

1 'How I began', *TP's weekly*, xxi(6 June 1913), 707.

2 The most useful studies of the work include N C de Nagy, *The poetry of Ezra Pound: the pre-Imagist stage* (Bern, 1960); T H Jackson, *The early poetry of Ezra Pound* (Cambridge, Mass, 1968); and Hugh Witemayer, *The poetry of Ezra Pound: forms and renewals 1908-1920* (Los Angeles and Berkeley, 1969).

3 This is probably the sense in which *Personae* (1909) could later be described by Pound as a series of poems, in each of which he had cast off a 'mask of the self' (GB, 85), although such a description must to a large extent be thought of as Vorticist revision.

4 *Biographia literaria*, ed J Shawcross (London, 1907), ii, 243. Coleridge in turn was referring to Plotinus's *Enneads* I on the power of the soul to recognise intuitively its kinship with divine beauty.

5 See *Longinus on the sublime*, ed and trans W Rhys Roberts (Cambridge, 1939), xiii, 81.

6 Letter to Harriet Monroe (15 September 1914), Harper Memorial Library, Chicago.

7 See especially 'Raphaelite Latin', *Book news monthly*, xxv (Philadelphia, Sept 1906), 31-4; 'Burgos, a dream city of old Castile', *Book news monthly*, xxv(October 1906), 91-4; and 'M Antonius Flaminius and John Keats, a kinship in genius, *Book news monthly*, xxvi(February 1908), 445-7.

8 *Longinus on the sublime*, i, 43.

9 This image reappeared in Pound's definition of the organic, non-mimetic nature of the Vorticist work (GB, 146-7).

10 These were among the 'great critics' on whom Pound gave his introductory lecture, in January 1909, for his course on 'The development of literature in Southern Europe' — lectures from which *The spirit of romance* was developed. In this and other lists of the same period, Pound also mentioned Plato, Aristotle, De Quincy and Yeats. See Noel Stock, *The life of Ezra Pound* (London, 1970), p58, and Letters, 42.

138

11 For biographical information, see Noel Stock, *The life of Ezra Pound*; additional materials in Hugh Kenner's *The Pound era* (Berkeley and Los Angeles, 1971). Charles Norman's *Ezra Pound* (New York, 1960) is less reliable.

12 (London, 1904); see ppx-xi.

13 Thus quoted in SR, 50, and remembered in the 1915 essay 'Remy de Gourmont', SPr, 384; compare *Biographia literaria*, pp15f.

14 *Op cit*

15 'Vortex', BLAST, i(20 June 1914), 153.

16 The phallic development of this moral energy, which Pound discusses in his notes to his translation of Remy de Gourmont's *The natural philosophy of love* (New York, 1922), pp206-19, pervades the *Cantos* in the form of a male energy which shapes female chaos. For a Lacanian analysis of this aspect, see Alan Durant, *Ezra Pound: identity in crisis* (Brighton, 1981) pp96ff, who traces this ideological strand into Pound's fascist conclusions.

17 'Brevora', *Little review*, v(October 1918), 23.

18 See for example 'Burgos, dream city of old Castile', *Book news monthly*, xxv(October 1906), 91-4.

19 SR, 26-38, both translations and textual comments.

20 Pound's title for this series of anthology-essays refers to the myth of Osiris, who spread civilisation among the barbarians, was torn to pieces, gathered, and resurrected: this is Pound's image for the critical task of retrieving valid details and renewing them within a vital body of art.

21 Letters, 140-41; also in 'How to read', LE, 29; ABC, 71, etc.

22 *Criterion*, i(January 1923), 148.

23 'Praefatio', *Active anthology* (London, 1933), pp24, 26.

24 This, curiously, is consistent with the *phantastikon* image of the poem which Pound used in 'Plotinus' (ALS, 65) and 'Invern' (ALS, 55), and implied in other early poetry.

25 A general study of the ways in which material from the poetry of the past alters, recombines and is made-new in Pound's poetry would be an almost impossibly ambitious project. His reading and repeated re-use of poetic materials held in the memory was unending. One interesting approach, however, is in Hugh Kenner's *The Pound era* (Berkeley and Los Angeles, 1971) − see for example Kenner's discussion of Pound's use of Sappho, pp54ff.

II THE POET AS CRITIC

1 Donald Gallup, *A bibliography of Ezra Pound* (London, 1969); a new revision of this work is in progress.

2 (Paige, 153) Ezra Pound, letter to Isabel W Pound (February 23, 1910).

3 'Preface. by way of finale' in *Collected prose*, Folder 1 (Beinecke).

4 See for example his comments on notes in editions of Dante's poetry (LE, 208).

5 '*The quattro cento* by Adrian Stokes' [review], *Symposium*, iii (October 1932), 518.

6 'Dante and his Circle', in *Collected works of D G Rossetti*, (London, 1906), p33*n*.

7 See below, pp45-48.

8 Reprinted in *Pavannes and divisions* (New York, 1918).

9 *Active anthology* (London, [1933]), p237.

10 *Antheil and the Treatise on harmony* (Paris, 1924), p54.

11 Pound recognised this distinction in considering Ernest Fenollosa's methods (LE, 77).

12 See Pound's preface to George Oppen, *Discrete series* (New York, 1934), pv; also GK, 161.

13 'Past history', *English journal* (Coll Edn), xxii(May, 1933) 356.

14 See 'The island of Paris, a letter, November 1920', *Dial*, lxix (December 1920), 636; and also 'Modern Georgics', LE, 384. As an example of such positive attention with a refusal to make general evaluations, note 'Hark to Sturge Moore', *Poetry*, vi(June 1915), 139-45, especially p139.

15 For example, 'Books current: Henry James as expositor', *Future*, ii(April 1918), 130.

16 'Hark to Sturge Moore', p142.

17 'Studies in contemporary mentality ... ix', *New age*, xxi (18 October 1917), 528, and many similar statements elsewhere.

18 'Excernment' seems to be Pound's own formulation of a noun from the obsolete verb 'excern' (*ex- -cernere*, L, to sift) which means 'excrete'. The verb was used in biological contexts, but Pound was apparently making a back-formation to the Latin root.

19 Preface, *Active anthology*, p11.

20 Ed Ezra Pound and Marcella Spann, (New York, 1964), which examines a poetic tradition in terms of technical verse-history, and in whose preface Pound re-states the need for the student to learn the book's 'meaning' by examining the significant documents which it contains.

21 (Paige, no 1126) letter, Pound to W W Hatfield (23 April, 1934).

22 *Active anthology*, p11; compare T S Eliot, 'Tradition and the individual talent', *Selected essays 1917-1932* (London, 1932), p15.

23 *Latin literature* (London, 1895): see (Paige, no 11) letter by Pound to Homer L Pound (30 July, 1909).

24 Preface, *Active anthology*, pp5, 10-11.

25 See 'Homage to Propertius', *New age*, xxvi(4 Dec. 1919), 82-3; and 'Practical suggestions', *Poetry*, xxxiii(March 1929), 332-3. I shall argue that the claim is probably not wholly justified.

26 See Michael Alexander, *The poetic achievement of Ezra Pound*, (London and Boston, 1979), pp66-79. for a sound analysis of the poem; also Donald Davie, *Ezra Pound: the poet as sculptor* (London, 1965), pp24-7.

27 The poem is an 'impression' or imitation in English of a text in another language; see Hugh Witemayer, *The poetry of Ezra Pound: forms and renewals* (Los Angeles and Berkeley, 1969), pp144-5.

28 See the editorial notes to 'Homage to Quintus Sextus F Christianus', *Poetry*, viii(September 1916), 329.

29 For further discussion, see Hugh Kenner, *The Pound era* (Berkeley and Los Angeles, 1973), pp82-9.

30 There are good discussions of this mode of translation in L S Dembo, *The Confucian odes of Ezra Pound* (London, 1963), and 'The women of Trachis: a symposium', *Pound newsletter*, v(January 1955), 3-8.

31 J P Sullivan, 'Ezra Pound and the classics', in *New approaches to Ezra Pound*, ed Eva Hesse (London 1969), p225; also see pp215-41 *passim*, and (in a different context) Massimo Bacigalupo, *The formed trace* (New York, 1980), pp181-218.

32 These notebooks are found in the Pound Archive at the Beinecke Library, Yale; see Poetry notebooks, nos 15-26; see also Pound's comments (LE, 182-91). My view of Pound's attitude to the texts is supported by the comments of James E Shaw, *Guido Cavalcanti's Theory of love* (Toronto, 1949), pp212-3, but is not accepted by all commentators: see George M Gugelberger, *Ezra Pound's medievalism* (Frankfurt, Bern, Las Vegas, 1978) pp96-8.

33 'Views and reviews: Binyon's Purgatorio', *New English weekly*, xiii(29 September 1938), 373.

34 This argument has been skirted by a number of scholars and probably by many translators, but it seems to have been first fully understood in the context of Pound's practice by Donald David, *Ezra Pound: the poet as sculptor*, pp12-13.

35 In Pound Archive, Beinecke; Poetry notebooks 42-59, dated April 1 1946, to January 19 1947, record his work on the Odes.

36 One of many examples can be found in the succession of versions of poem no 170, Notebooks 44, 45, 52, 57.

37 Poetry notebook 48, p60 *verso*.

38 See 'The teacher's mission' (1934), LE, 58-63; the essay is an updating of 'The serious artist' (1913), LE, 41-57, and is related to 'Date line' (also 1934), LE, 74-87; the three should therefore be read in conjunction.

39   Letter, Pound to Viola Scott Jordan [October 1907] (Beinecke).

40   The phrase occurs in the first paragraph of the work which Pound cited as his source: Rodolphi Agricola Phrisii, *Dialectica (De inuentione dialectica libri tres)* (Lowanii, 1515); although Pound apparently owned a copy of the book, and in a letter to his mother in 1925 named it as one of his books which she should keep for him rather than dispose of, there is no evidence that he had read more than the first page.

41   See Chapter III.

42   'Affirmations, ii: Vorticism', *New age*, xvi(14 Jan. 1915) 278).

43   See 'Wyndham Lewis', *Egoist*, i(15 June 1914), 234.

44   See for example the change of emphasis between statements in 'Editorial', *Little review*, iv(May 1917), 6, and 'Murder by capital', *Criterion*, xii(July 1933), 590-9.

45   Hueffer's book, *Memories and impressions* (New York and London, 1911), gives a good idea of the way in which his cultural élitism may have appeared in the conversations between Hueffer, Pound, and others of their circle. Pound of course always emphasised Hueffer's influence on himself.

46   'Wyndham Lewis', *Egoist*, i(5 June 1914), 233-4).

47   The latter resembles the idea of poetry as 'nutrition of impulse'. Five years later, however, in writing about Henry James, Pound was inclined to equate poetry with the positive, and prose with the negative in his system; see LE, 324*n*.

48   See below, pp65ff.

49   *How to teach reading: a primer for Ezra Pound* (Cambridge, 1932).

50   *Jefferson and/or Mussolini* (New York [1936]), p15 and *passim*; and letter to Peter Russell [September 1949] in the Lockwood Memorial Library, University of Buffalo.

51   Hueffer's book, *Henry James* (London, 1913) also stressed the role of the novelist as objective critic of society.

52   Only the essay written in French for the *Mercure de France* (1922) deals with such technical matters as thematic form in *Ulysses*, and linguistic usages; this may have been a specific attempt to convince a critically well-educated French audience of the real value of the work by even the highest (French) criteria. This and other material relating to Joyce may be consulted in *Pound/Joyce*, ed Forrest Read (New York, 1967).

53   (Paris, 1923); see Pound's remarks on James, LE, 296-7.

54   See especially Pound's comments on Tarr's attack on Hobson (LE, 427-8).

55   *De vulgari eloquentia*; i, p146; ii, pp162, 164.

56   See for example 'E E Cummings alive', *New English weekly* vi(13 December 1934), 210.

57 See the argument of 'How to read' (LE, 31), where Pound describes serious writing as 'going over' from poetry to prose at a certain point in literary history.

58 This is the message of 'The wisdom of poetry' (SPr, 330-31); but the concept is repeated in a number of other contexts, of which 'How to read' (1929) (LE, 21) is a prominent later example.

59 GK, 16; *Confucian analects*, trans Pound (London, 1956), p79.

60 'James Joyce' (1917), in *Pound/Joyce*, p90.

61 See 'Debabelisation and Ogden', *New English weekly*, vi (28 Feb 1935), 410-11.

62 'For a new Paideuma', (1938) (S Pr, 254-8).

III TEXT AND FORM

1 *Confucius*, trans, commentary Ezra Pound (New York, 1969) p20.

2 'Editorial on solicitous doubt', *Little review*, iv(October 1917), 22.

3 'Past history', *English journal (College edn.)*, xxii (May 1933), 352. See also material from *Lustra* (1916), especially the items originally published in 1913 under the title 'Contemporania' (CSP, 91-4, 97-8, 99, 119).

4 'Exhibition at the Goupil Gallery', *Egoist*, i(16 March 1914), 109.

5 'The approach to Paris, v' *New age*, xiii(2 October 1913), 662.

6 Letters, 91 and 91n. T H Jackson in *The early poetry of Ezra Pound* (Cambridge, Mass., 1968), 75-6, relates this demand to Pound's search for a poetry of contemplation, in which the mind is mystically unified with the object of its attention.

7 'Ford Madox Hueffer', *New freewoman*, 1(15 Dec. 1913), 251.

8 See below, pp66ff.

9 John Gould Fletcher, in 'Three Imagist Poets', *Little review*, iii(May 1916), 30, defined the presentation of a thing as an image, as 'the sum-total of the emotions in any given subject', presented 'in such a way that the reader experiences the self-same emotions from them'. He was arguing that sensual stimulation causes the reader to recreate imaginatively the emotional complex out of which the poem arose. Fletcher's version of the 'image' is more consistent than Pound's, being a simple conjunction of Romantic, expressive and organic criteria.

10 'The approach to Paris, v', *New age*, xiii(2 October 1913), 662.

11 An account of this struggle is given in Jackson, *The early poetry of Ezra Pound*, pp119-85.

12 'Correspondence', *Poetry*, vii(March 1916), 322.

13 *Antheil and the Treatise on harmony* (Chicago, 1927), p38.

14   *How to teach reading: a primer for Ezra Pound* (Cambridge, 1932) especially p14.

15   Translations, 23; also letter from Pound to Viola Scott Jordan (18 October 1907) (Beinecke).

16   Longinus, *On the sublime*, xxxix, 143-5.

17   'Prologomena' (1913), LE, 8-12; Northrop Frye, in his Introduction (pp x-xxv) to *Sound and poetry*, English Inst Essays, 1956 (New York, 1957), discusses the analogies between music and literature in a very helpful way, beginning with Aristotelian *melos* and *lexis*, and throwing considerable light on Pound's *melopoeia*.

18   See below, pp78ff.

19   This was interpreted by many, from Amy Lowell to the current Pound student, as a demand for free verse. However we have already seen that, as with the two previous 'rules', it was part of a general programme for expressive efficiency.

20   The reading strategy can be heard quite clearly in *Ezra Pound reading his poetry* (New York: Caedmon, 1960); the search for a quantitative metre is made clear in his discussion of *vers libre* in 'A retrospect', LE, 12-13.

21   'Mr Pound replies to Mr Tate', *Poetry*, xli (January 1933), 231.

22   Letter, Pound to Peter Russell (ca June 1950) (Lockwood Memorial Library, Buffalo).

23   *De vulgari eloquentia*, ii, 188.

24   'Music', *New age*, xxiv(7 November 1918), 11-12; ABC, 152.

25   See for example Pound's recitation of 'Cantico del sole' (CSP, 202), on *Ezra Pound reading his poetry* (New York, Caedmon, 1960).

26   See *Antheil and the Treatise on harmony* (Chicago, 1927), pp11-14; and LE, 431-9, 155, etc.

27   ABC, 202-3; and *Antheil and the Treatise on harmony*, pp204-5.

28   *De vulgari eloquentia*, ii, 196-248.

29   'Tagore's Poems', *Poetry*, i(December 1912), 92.

30   Murray Schafer, ed, *Ezra Pound and music* (New York, 1977); see especially pp467-80. The volume incorporates material by 'William Atheling' as well as Pound's own more theoretical work.

31   *Antheil and the Treatise on harmony*, especially pp9-10.

32   'The island of Paris. A letter. November 1920', *Dial*, lxix (December 1920), 638.

33   'The approach to Paris, vii., *New age*, xiii(16 October 1913), 8.

34   'Vortex', BLAST, 1(20 June 1914), 153; GB, 93; the attitude, however, is foreshadowed in discussions of music in the 1911-12 'Osiris' essays.

35   See below, pp78ff.

36   For Pound's attitude to these developments, see Letters, 77-9. 84-5, and especially 90.

37 Pound himself used the forms 'Imagiste' and 'Imagisme' especially at the beginning, probably to suggest that this was something as serious as a French literary movement. The '-e' is normally omitted by commentators, and always in relation to Amy Lowell's continuations of the *Imagist anthology.*

On one or two occasions, Pound used 'imagism' as a synonym for 'phanopoeia', but that is a confusing, and I think meaningless usage (GB, 95). Considerable critical attention has been focused on both the Imagist Movement and Pound's Imagism. While this suggests something of the confusions and problems which have been caused by Imagism, the reader will find considerable critical material of help and interest; probably Herbert Schneidau's study of Imagist poetics in *Ezra Pound: the image and the real* (Baton Rouge, 1969), Donald Davie's *Ezra Pound: the poet as sculptor* (London, 1965), Hugh Kenner, *The Pound era* (Berkeley and Los Angeles, 1971), and Cairns Craig, *Yeats, Eliot, Pound and the politics of poetry* (London and Canberra, 1982) are the best volumes to consult.

38 Quoted in Cairns Craig, *Yeats, Eliot, Pound and the politics of poetry*, p58.

39 T E Hulme, *Speculations*, ed Herbert Read (London, 1924), pp133-4; also 'Lecture on modern poetry' and 'Notes on language and style', in Michael Roberts, *T E Hulme* (London, 1938), pp258ff and 117n. See also A R Jones, 'Imagisme: a unity of gesture', *American poetry*, ed I Ehrenpreis, (Stratford-on-Avon Studies, 7, 1965), pp116-7.

40 T E Hulme, 'Searchers after reality', *New age*, v(19 August 1909), 315. Beside his description of words as counters — Pound did not adopt the pejorative sense — Hulme seems to have contributed less to Pound's Imagism than past scholars have often suggested.

41 'Vorticism', *Fortnightly review*, xcvi (1 Sept. 1914), 461-2.

42 ... unless this is what Pound meant by Dante's 'extended comparison' (SR, 157-9).

43 *TP's weekly*, xxv(20 February, 1915), 185.

44 Quoted by Wallace Martin, 'Freud and Imagism', *Notes and queries*, viii(December 1961), 47.

45 *Poetry*, ii(April 1913), 12; see GB, 101.

46 See David Lodge, *The modes of modern writing* (London, 1977).

47 R E Smith, 'Ezra Pound and the haiku', *College English*, xxvi (April 1965), 523, points out that the conventional haiku moves from the natural and particular to the human and general. For the influence of haiku on Imagism, see Earl Miner, *The Japanese tradition in British and American literature* (Princeton, 1966), pp98-107.

48 Letter from Pound to Isabel W Pound (19 Sept 1909), (Paige, no 122).

49   *A Lume Spento 1908-1958* (Milano, 1958), p37.

50   SR, 222, 127-8; S Pr, 24-8, 329-32, etc.

51   'Affirmations ii: Vorticism', *New age*, xvi(14 Jan 1915), 277.

52   'Ezra Pound: an interview', *Paris review*, vii(Summer/Fall 1962), 30; also GB, 155-7.

53   Timothy Materer, *Vortex: Pound, Eliot, Lewis* (Ithaca and London, 1979) is an informative work on this material.

54   However, according to 'Long live the Vortex', BLAST, 1 (20 June 1914), 7, Futurism (like Impressionism and Naturalism) was a mimetic mode; see also GB, 104.

55   See Wyndham Lewis, *Time and western man* (London, 1927), pp 54-5; 'Those were the days', in *Imagist anthology 1930* ed Glenn Hughes (New York, 1930, pp ix-xii; Horace Brodzky, *Henri Gaudier-Brzeska* (London, 1933), pp99-100. Further information may be found in Materer, and also in Ronald Bush, *The genesis of Ezra Pound's Cantos* (Princeton, 1976), pp21-52.

56   *De Quincey's literary criticism* (London, 1909), p168; cp Letters, 65, for Pound's use of the term in 1913. In the same essay de Quincey wrote that a period of cultural creativity is succeeded by one of reflection, imitation, and finally 'the sense of oppression from inimitable models', a cyclical view of literary history which resembles that of Pound's 'How to read' (LE, 33) and may have shaped it.

57   LE, 44; confirmed in a letter to Harriet Monroe (1914), in the Harriet Monroe collection of the University of Chicago.

58   PE, 51. In the later prose and the *Cantos*, 'light' is a (Neoplatonic) symbol for the creative power of the intellect; its resemblance to early *virtù*, the vortex pattern, and the creative imagination should be noted.

59   'Affirmations, ii: Vorticism', *New age*, xvi(14 January 1915), 277.

60   Ibid.

61   LE, 154-5; compare Canto 74/449. See Walter Baumann, *The Rose in the steel-dust* (Bern, 1967), pp15-16, 161-70.

62   'Vortex', BLAST, 1(June 20, 1914), 153. The passage is reminiscent of both W B Yeats's essay 'The symbolism of poetry' in *Essays and introductions* (London, 1961), pp156-7, and Pater's essay 'On style', with its statement about the arts aspiring to the 'condition of music': *Appreciations* (London, 1889), p37.

63   (London, 1910), pp130-54, and especially 130-31.

64   'Affirmations, ii: Vorticism', *New age*, xvi(Jan 14, 1915), 277.

65   This at least is how I would interpret his statement that such elements might, in a play, hinder the 'poetry' of the work (ABC, 46-7).

66   'Notes to Bibi-la-Bibiste', *Little review*, vii(September-October 1924), 24.

67   'Vortex', BLAST, 1(20 June 1914), 153.

68   For the suggestion that words should be seen as the names of

objects and properties, see T E Hulme's 'Lecture on modern poetry', in Michael Roberts, *T E Hulme* (London, 1938), p266. Pound's theory of form allows abstractions as well as objects and enlarges the field of poetic reference.

69 See below, pp119ff.

IV KNOWLEDGE AND THE *CANTOS*

1 When, in *The spirit of romance*, Pound wrote of the simultaneity of work within the literary tradition, he implied the view that each newly-written work takes its place intertextually (SR, 8). The point is made even more clearly in T S Eliot's Poundian essay, 'Tradition and the individual talent'.

2 See *Antheil and the Treatise on harmony* (Chicago, 1927), pp32-3.

3 *Ibid*, pp44-5.

4 'Wyndham Lewis', *Egoist*, i(June 15 1914), 233-4; 'Editorial', *little review*, iv(May 1917), 4-6.

5 See 'America, chances and remedies, v', *New age*, xiii(5 June, 1913), 143; 'The approach to Paris', 7 parts, *New age*, xiii (4 Sept-16 Oct 1913). See also Warren Ramsey, 'Pound, Laforgue and dramatic structure', *Comparative literature*, iii(Winter 1951), 50 and *passim*.

6 Compare Remy de Gourmont, *Le problème du style* (Paris, 1907), p105.

7 The rupture of relationships between Pound and Harriet Monroe (editor of *Poetry*) was a consequence of the first of the attacks on his work by Professor W G Hale. For a full and definitive account of *Propertius* and its problems, see J P Sullivan, *Ezra Pound and Propertius* (London, 1965); a classical scholar, Sullivan finally demolished the argument that Pound's translation is merely ignorant.

8 At least, it was usually unknown, although the aim is directly stated in the epigraph to 'Sestina: Altaforte' (CSP, 42). And see 'Histrion', ALS, 108.

9 'Homage to Sextus Propertius', *New age*, xxvi(4 Dec 1919), 83; the letter, quoted in J P Sullivan, pp8-10, reveals much of Pound's method and purpose.

10 See MIN, pp187-8; and 'The approach to Paris, ii', *New age*, xiii(11 Sept 1913), 577-9.

11 The most recent and detailed study is in Richard Sieburth, *Instigations: Ezra Pound and Remy de Gourmont* (Cambridge, Mass; and London, 1978).

12 The main reference here is Gourmont's essay 'La dissociation des idées' in *La culture des idées* (Paris, 1916), pp69-106; see p69.

147

13　See below, p108.

14　For an account of the process of revision, see Terri Brint Joseph, '"Near Perigord": a perplexity of voice', *Paideuma*, xi(Spring 1982), 93-8.

15　Useful discussions of this function will be found in Roland Barthes, *Image-music-text*, ed and trans Stephen Heath (London, 1977), pp142-8; and Michel Foucault, 'What is an author', trans Kari Hanet, *Screen*, xx(1979), 13-33.

16　Pound's argument in 'As for Imagisme' (S Pr, 344-7) is relevant to this point.

17　If we consider the *Cantos* as discourse, the subjective subsection of the *Pisan cantos* merely plays a role, with respect to the work as a whole, analogous to that of section III of 'Near Perigord'.

18　See Barthes and Foucault, *op cit*. The ancestry of this conception of textual impersonality is a study large enough to require another monograph stretching from French Symbolisme to Eliot's 'Tradition and the individual talent'. Arthur Symons's quotation of Mallarmé (in *The symbolist movement in literature, q* Hugh Kenner, *The Pound era* (Berkeley and Los Angeles, 1973), pp136-7, is worth placing beside Barthes: 'The pure work implies the elocutionary disappearance of the poet, who yields place to the words, immobilised by the shock of the inequality; they take light from mutual reflection, like an actual train of fire over previous stones, replacing the old lyric afflatus or the enthusiastic personal direction of the phrase.' For a discussion of mediaeval contexts in which Pound himself may have become aware of the idea of multiple authorship, see Georg M Gugelberger, *Ezra Pound's medievalism*, European University Papers, Ser xviii (Frankfurt, Bern, Las Vegas, 1978), pp25-7. This is of course the subject of the 'Ur-Cantos'.

19　Massimo Bacigalupo, in *The formed trace* (New York, 1980), p7, calls them 'those uninhibited confessions of a "beautiful soul"'. With the exception of the *Pisan cantos*, they are the last consistently-authorial poetic statement Pound made.

20　A series of drafts and notes for the version of seven cantos preceding the present accepted text is filed in the Pound Archive (Beinecke).

21　Ronald Bush, *The genesis of Ezra Pound's Cantos* (Princeton, 1976), p56.

22　See especially J P Sullivan, *Ezra Pound and Propertius* (London, 1965), pp35-76.

23　Quoted by Noel Stock, *The life of Ezra Pound* (London, 1970), p224.

24　The titlepage to *Hugh Selwyn Mauberley* (see *Personae: the collected poems of Ezra Pound*, 1926, p[185]) read: 'The sequence is so directly a farewell to London that the reader who chooses to regard
148

this as an exclusively American edition may as well omit it and turn at once to page 205.'

25 The line is a misquotation of Villon's 'L'an trentièsme'; the alteration in itself makes the reference autobiographical.

26 *Ezra Pound's Mauberley* (London, 1955).

27 The quality of a written text which is often called 'tone' is notoriously difficult to judge, and is the cause of much difficulty in interpreting Pound's work. It can often be illuminated by a poet's reading of his work. In this case, Pound's recorded reading (*Ezra Pound reads his poetry*, New York, Caedmon Records, 1958) is variable and uncertain in vocal intonation.

28 (London, 1979), pp201-4.

29 See J J Espey, *Ezra Pound's Mauberley*, pp77-8.

30 There is a variant typescript in the Pound collection at the library of Hamilton College, NY.

31 Compare Pound's preface to Lionel Johnson's *Poetical works* (London, 1915) (LE, 361-70); the reader may wish to speculate on the importance of Johnson as a model for Mauberley himself.

32 Compare GB, 103. An excellent discussion of the critical function of the poem is in R P Blackmur, *Language as gesture* (London, 1955), pp125-36.

33 See Hugh Kenner, 'The broken mirrors and the mirror of memory', *English Institute essays 1953* (London, 1955), pp15-7.

34 'The approach to Paris, v', *New age*, xiii(2 Oct 1913), 662.

35 Letters, 218. '*Constater*', with its context and significance, is adopted from Hueffer, who used it of a 'method of presentation' in *The critical attitude* (London, 1911), p35.

36 'The approach to Paris, v', p662.

37 'Pastiche. The Regional, vii', *New age*, xxv(21 August, 1919), 284. This piece marks the first appearance of Pound's social comment in the epigrammatic later style.

38 'Epstein, Belgion and Meaning', *Criterion*, ix(April, 1930, 475.

39 See for example Hugh Kenner, *The Pound era*, pp68-9; and LE,61.

40 'The new therapy', *New age*, xx(16 March 1922), 259-60 (a review of relevant work). Under the influence of Gourmont and Louis Berman, Pound made a pseudo-scientific explanation of the ideogrammic event in physiological terms, describing a moment of understanding, or 'original thought', as the product of a sudden glandular change which causes new juxtapositions of fact.

41 Ernest Fenollosa, *The Chinese written character as a medium for poetry* (Washington, DC, 1951), pp76-7; ABC, 22 and 17-18.

42 I find it difficult to take Pound's gestures toward scientific knowledge seriously. In the development of his poetic, his patchy knowledge of the sciences seems to me to have the status of a body of

images and analogies used strategically to lend an air of the 'real', the 'serious' and the 'modern' to poetic matters. If he sometimes fooled himself about what he was doing — as for example in swallowing Gourmont's 'physiology' and disgorging it into sexual mysticism — this may affect the connotational interpretation of his work in ways outside the scope of an aesthetic study. In this judgement I am unrepentantly at odds with much of the interesting study of Ian Bell, *Critic as scientist: the modernist poetics of Ezra Pound* (New York and London, 1981), except of course for his final chapter.

43 *Speculations*, ed Herbert Read (London, 1924), pp180-1; the fact that Pound described Bergson as 'crap' in 'This Hulme business', *Townsman*, ii (January 1939), 15, I take as confirming rather than denying that he was exposed by Hulme to Bergsonian concepts.

44 Fenollosa, especially pp62-9, 78-80. See also Laurence W Chisholm, *Fenellosa: the Far East and American culture* (New Haven and London, 1963), p216.

45 Fenollosa, pp13-14.

46 Both Fenollosa and Pound seem to have known about the sound element and chose to ignore it: see Hugh Kenner, *The Pound era* (Berkeley and Los Angeles, 1973), pp227-9.

47 It is hard to believe that the phrasing is not Pound's, since it echoes Hulme's term in his statement that every word should be 'an image *seen*, not a *counter*', and that prose is just such a juggling of counters in patterns worn by over-use: see Michael Roberts, *T E Hulme* (London, 1938), pp274, 272.

48 See 'Mr Pound and his poetry', *Athenaeum*, xciii (31 Oct 1919), 1132.

49 'Vortex', BLAST, i(20 June, 1914), 153.

50 In Hulme's translation of Bergson's *An introduction to metaphysics* (London, 1913), pp14-15, this associational method is presented as a means of destroying conventional mental habits, a theme of Pound's writing from the years of Vorticism onward. Bergson's formulation here of the psychology and philosophy of French symbolism on the basis of association results in a 'symbol' which Pound's ideogram closely resembles.

51 To misunderstand this is to take literally Pound's claims as a historian, assume that the later poetry is in fact mimetic, and object to its literal inaccuracies. To complain of Pound that 'he did not examine the records as a historian; he did not question them against other records and the writings of historians' (see Noel Stock, *Poet in exile*, Manchester, 1964, p182) is a correct observation, but implies an unquestioning acceptance of representational interpretative criteria for the poetry, and of Pound's own most inflated claims. Whether this is a fruitful approach to any poetry seems rather doubtful.

52 Quoted in *Impact*, ed Noel Stock (Chicago, 1960), p198; and
150

see also remarks on the weakness of Western ratiocinative methods, GK, 27-8.

53 *Pound/Joyce*, ed Forrest Read (New York, 1970), pp193-4; and 'On criticism in general' *Criterion*, i(Jan 1923), 143-56.

54 All references are to typescript versions in the folders *Three cantos I* and *Three cantos II* (Beinecke), containing transcripts of autograph and typescript mss, and the folder *Ur-Cantos unpublished* containing less finished materials. For an account of the developement of the 'Ur-Cantos' and convenient reprints of some material, see Ronald Bush, *The genesis of Ezra Pound's Cantos* (Princeton, 1976).

55 T S Eliot, 'Ezra Pound', *Today*, iv(September 1918), 6-7; 'The method of Mr Pound', *Athenaeum*, xciii(24 Oct 1919), 1065; and see Ronald Bush, pp4-5 and 142-82.

56 For example, 'An introduction to the economic nature of the United States' (1944), in *Impact*, p15, and Letters, 285.

57 Quoted in Noel Stock, *The life of Ezra Pound* (London, 1970), pp184, 289.

58 'Mr Ezra Pound's *Cantos*', *New English weekly*, iii(May 11, 1933), 96, quoted in Ronald Bush, pp13-14.

59 See Roland Barthes, *The pleasures of the text*, trans R Miller (London, 1976), pp75-6; also Pierre Machery, *A theory of literary production*, trans G Wall (London, 1978). Such a withholding seems implicit in Pound's various promises that the *Cantos* would contain about a hundred poems (Letters, 247, 321) and his promise of an exegesis if the meaning did not at that point become transparent (Letters, 418).

60 See A Alvarez, *The shaping spirit* (London, 1958), p60.

61 *Poetry notebooks*, nos 32 to 39 incl (Beinecke).

62 *Poetry notebooks*, nos 15-26 incl (Beinecke).

63 *Poetry notebooks*, no 28 [1936] (Beinecke).

64 *Poetry notebooks*, no 35 (Beinecke).

65 The appearance of dialect passages in the *Cantos* is obviously on some occasions the record of a simple memory; but in others the material seems invented and structurally misplaced. It is worth noting that Pound was interested in Joyce's use of dialect in *Ulysses*, which he admired as a means of rapid 'presentation' of 'tones of mind': see *Pound/Joyce*, ed Forrest Read (New York, 1970, pp195-6.

66 Donald Davie, *Ezra Pound: the poet as sculptor* (London, 1965), pp204-6.

67 See also *Cantos*, 7/27.

68 *The Pound era*, p535.

69 Pound himself was probably concerned in this, as in so much else, to discriminate rather than evaluate. In an early draft, he wrote that at this point the 'thin clear stuff gives way before the . . . florid phrase'.

70 *Sailing after knowledge* (London, 1963), p153.

INDEX